mySAP.com
Industry Solutions

Other titles in the series

Flying Start with SAP R/3 by Gabriele Schicht and Andrea Schmieden
SAP R/3 Quality Management by Michael Hölzer and Michael Schramm
SAP R/3 Plant Maintenance by Britta Stengl and Reinhard Ematinger
SAP R/3 Financial Accounting by Sandra Brinkmann and Axel Zeilinger
Security and Data Protection with SAP Systems by Werner Hornberger and
   Jürgen Schneider

mySAP.com
Industry Solutions

New strategies for success with
SAP's Industry Business Units

Prof Dr Henning Kagermann and Dr Gerhard Keller

an imprint of **Pearson Education**

Harlow, England • London • New York • Reading, Massachusetts • San Francisco • Toronto • Don Mills, Ontario •
Sydney • Tokyo • Singapore • Hong Kong • Seoul • Taipei • Cape Town • Madrid • Mexico City • Amsterdam •
Munich • Paris • Milan

PEARSON EDUCATION LIMITED

Head Office:
Edinburgh Gate
Harlow
Essex CM20 2JE
Tel: +44 (0)1279 623623
Fax: +44 (0)1279 431059

London Office:
128 Long Acre
London WC2E 9AN
Tel: +44 (0)20 7447 2000
Fax: +44 (0)20 7240 5771

Website: www.informit.uk.com
www.aw.com/cseng/

First published in Great Britain in 2001

© Galileo Press GmbH 2000

The rights of Henning Kagermann and Gerhard Keller to be identified as Authors of this Work have been asserted by them in accordance with the Copyright, Designs and Patents Act 1988.

ISBN 0-201-72192-9

British Library Cataloguing in Publication Data
A CIP catalogue record for this book can be obtained from the British Library

Library of Congress Cataloging in Publication Data
SAP-Branchenlösungen. English
    mySAP.com industry solutions/Henning Kagermann and Gerhard Keller [editors].
        p. cm.
    Includes bibliographical references and index.
    ISBN 0-201-72192-9
        1. SAP AG. 2. mySAP.com 3. Business–Computer programs. 4. Industrial management–Computer programs. I. Kagermann, Henning. II. Keller, Gerhard. III. Title.

    HF5548.4.R2 S262 2001
    650′.0285′53769–dc21   2001020195

The programs in this book have been included for their instructional value. The publisher does not offer any warranties or representations in respect of their fitness for a particular purpose, nor does the publisher accept any liability for any loss or damage arising from their use.

Many of the designations used by manufacturers and sellers to distinguish their products are claimed as trademarks. Pearson Education Limited has made every attempt to supply trademark information about manufacturers and their products mentioned in this book. A list of trademark designations and their owners appears on this page.

Trademark Notice
All of the screenshots and graphics reproduced in this book are subject to copyright © SAP AG, Neurottstr. 16, 69190 Walldorf, Germany. SAP, R/3, R/2, Accelerated SAP, SAP PRESS, mySAP.com and SAP Industry Solutions are trademarks or registered trademarks of SAP AG, Walldorf, Germany.

10 9 8 7 6 5 4 3 2 1

Designed by Claire Brodmann Book Designs, Lichfield, Staffs.
Typeset by M Rules, London, UK.
Printed and bound in Great Britain by Biddles Ltd.

The Publishers' policy is to use paper manufactured from sustainable forests.

Contents

12   mySAP SERVICE PROVIDERS INDUSTRY SOLUTION   150

Foreword

SAP AG introduced mySAP.com in the summer of 1999 to align its products, processes and structures with the Internet. The introduction marks a milestone in the logical, continuous and simultaneously consistent development of SAP AG. The central initiatives of this evolution in the past few years include strict orientation toward industries and a focus on user-friendly interfaces with EnjoySAP.

This series of books seeks to describe the link between the intensive industry-orientation of SAP over the past two years and mySAP.com. It brings home the concrete relationships between mySAP.com and the mySAP.com Industry Solutions to SAP customers and partners as well as to all those working in the SAP environment.

The development of mySAP.com looked back to previous experience gained in the context of the industry strategy. For example, the orientation of SAP toward industries required intensive examination of industry-specific, professional roles, and mapping those roles in each industry solution. As a result, the delivery of mySAP.com in July 2000 provides 142 cross-industry and 75 industry-specific roles.

The task of this first volume in the series on mySAP.com Industry Solutions therefore provides an overview of the continuity of SAP as it undergoes change. Additional books on selected, individual industries will follow this overview. For example, this first edition selected 11 industries that can illustrate the demands of the new Internet age on SAP and its customers. We hope that a future edition of this overview volume will cover all 20 currently available mySAP.com Industry Solutions.

This first book in the series contains a collection of articles on established Industry Solutions, such as mySAP Retail and mySAP Insurance, and newer solutions, such as mySAP Service Providers and mySAP Media.

All the chapters follow a similar structure. Each begins with an examination of the market trends to which each industry must react. A second section compares the requirements of the industry with the mySAP.com Industry Solution. Solution maps, developed collaboratively by SAP along with its customers and partners, assist in the comparison. The solution maps are based upon the most current development plans. To illustrate the benefits of the industry solutions, the closing section describes the concrete experience of customers.

A publishing project such as this cannot come to fruition without a great deal of help. We first wish to thank the authors who wrote the chapters. The knowledge provided in their contributions was important enough for them to sacrifice the meagre free time they had, given the demands of their diverse commitments.

We also wish to offer particular thanks to Christiane Feiler and Stefan Hack, who participated in conversations and discussions during the conceptual phase of this book. We wish to express our gratitude to Dr Marc Derungs, Hans-Jürgen Uhink and Werner Dilzer for their quality feedback on selected topics. For proofreading the articles, we thank Sven Köhler and Patric Beuthen. We wish to highlight the contribution of Frank Vollmer of Die Medienprofis, who edited the text. We owe special thanks to Bernhard Hochlehnert for initiating, designing and leading the overall project.

The editors
Prof Dr Henning Kagermann
Dr Gerhard Keller

Introduction

Bernhard Hochlehnert, SAP AG

THE DEVELOPMENT OF mySAP.com INDUSTRY SOLUTIONS

RIVA

Every idea has a source, and today's industry solutions from SAP have their roots in a development project that began in 1988. At that time, utilities companies using SAP R/2 on mainframe computers expressed the desire for a real-time information system for use in consumption billing. They had in mind a special solution tailored to the needs of power, gas and water suppliers, a solution that would probably prove inappropriate for most other industries. SAP responded to this request with the development of the RIVA component for R/2, a real time information system for consumption billing. It was the first industry-specific software solution developed by SAP.

Industry knowledge

Compared with the broad functional scope of today's industry solutions, the RIVA component could run both independently and as a satellite solution. Meanwhile, SAP broke new ground with this specialized solution. The developers soon saw that labour alone would not make the project succeed. It demanded an intensive examination of the core processes used in the utilities industry, and it demanded industry-specific knowledge.

Two industry solutions, SAP Oil & Gas and SAP Healthcare, started on SAP R/3 with its completely new client/server technology in 1991. This was based on a much broader functional foundation than RIVA. These developments also clarified the decisive role of industry-specific knowledge for the success of the product. It also became clear that a market existed for industry solutions.

Industry business units

Beginning in 1995, SAP created an organizational and personnel context for the overall structure of industry-specific, expert knowledge. The Industry Centres of Expertise (ICOE) originated in 1995, and SAP founded the Industry Business Units (IBUs) in 1998. The IBUs represent a consistent and complete orientation toward an industry. An IBU therefore holds responsibility not only for driving development on the part of SAP, but also for the development of add-ons and service offerings by partner companies.

SAP supplies a solution map for each industry solution. Solution maps illustrate the SAP elements, the add-ons and the services available in the solution. Specialists previously employed in the automobile industry, banking, insurance, retail or public service sectors work in each of the 13 current Industry Business Units responsible for one or more Industry Solutions. They know the peculiarities of each area, speak its language and follow developments in each industry. They are the catalysts for keeping mySAP.com Industry Solutions close to the market. SAP now offers some 20 industry solutions, the most recent being mySAP Mining. The table below lists the solutions currently available.

Industry Solutions

- mySAP Aerospace & Defense
- mySAP Automotive
- mySAP Banking
- mySAP Chemicals
- mySAP Consumer Products
- mySAP Engineering & Construction
- mySAP Healthcare
- mySAP High Tech
- mySAP Higher Education & Research
- mySAP Insurance
- mySAP Media
- mySAP Mill Products
- mySAP Mining
- mySAP Oil & Gas
- mySAP Pharmaceuticals
- mySAP Public Sector
- mySAP Retail
- mySAP Service Providers
- mySAP Telecommunications
- mySAP Utilities

mySAP.com   The SAP industry strategy shows that only consistent orientation toward the demands of the market leads to success. Industries will not become obsolete after the introduction of mySAP.com. They will continue to play a central role within the SAP strategy, and even expand it.

List of Contributors

Helen Apps graduated with a BA Honours degree in Tourism Management and Spanish from Leeds University in England in 1996. She started working for SAP AG in October 1997, and has been in Real Estate Product Management for the last two and a half years. Among a number of activities Helen is responsible for rollout and support of the real estate product in United Kingdom, Spain, Portugal, South Africa and the Nordic countries.

Dr Walter Bäckert studied chemical engineering at the ETH in Zurich, Switzerland and was then awarded a doctorate in systems engineering. At the same time, he also completed a degree in business at the University of Zurich. He worked for Ciba-Geigy for 15 years. During his last eight years there, he was a senior manager, responsible for global supply chain management and marketing, and lived in New York, California, and the Netherlands. Since July 1998, he has worked at IMG AG as the director of the global business unit for chemistry and life sciences. In that position, he holds responsibility for supply chain management and enterprise management.

Dr Roland Bürkle studied mathematics, physics and economics at the Universities of Stuttgart and Freiburg in Germany. He later earned a doctorate in business. Before moving to SAP in 1990, he worked in various capacities involving software development in the motor industry. At SAP he was responsible for the development of industry components for hospitals and publishing. In 1998 he became director of the newly-founded Industry Business Unit (iBU) Media.

Mario Burmeister studied business, majoring in business information services, and worked for the Lufthansa Group for 10 years. There he held responsibility for the marketing and sales portion of the SAP implementation project at Lufthansa Technik AG. During his first year at SAP, he was a consultant to the aviation industry, with a focus on invoicing. He is now responsible for the conceptual design of links between the SAP Project System (SAP PS) application component and the SAP solution for aviation.

Martin Elsner is a trained aviation technician and studied mechanical engineering, specialising in aircraft and space technology. After he graduated, he worked for three years at Deutsche Airbus AG and for two years at SAP Systems Integration AG as a consultant for the aviation industry, focusing on logistics. At SAP SI he is now responsible for module consulting, sub-project management, project reviews and scoping.

Dr Rainer Frei studied business at the University of Mannheim in Germany between 1988 and 1994, concentrating on industrial operations, international management and chemical technology. Between 1994 and 1998 he earned a doctorate in business and production at the Johannes Gutenberg University of Mainz, also in Germany. The subject of his dissertation was suppression management in the operations of the chemical industry with a heterogeneous production structure. Since 1998 he has worked as senior consultant for the chemical and pharmaceutical business unit at IMG AG. His consulting focus is on supply chain management and supply chain planning.

Manfred Gärtner trained in IT sales at Taylorix GmbH between 1982 and 1984; he then studied business in a career-enhancement programme at the Management and Economics Academy in Stuttgart in Germany. In 1988, he completed his studies with a degree in business management. After several positions as an application programmer and product manager for logistics, he took over project management for the development of the advertising management system, IS-M/AM, for the SAP Media solution. Since the beginning of 1998, he has been responsible for worldwide product management of the mySAP Media Industry Solution.

Reinhild Gefrerer is the director of the Metal, Paper and Wood Products IBU, and holds a degree in business management. Since 1998, she has held responsibility for the development and worldwide use of the mySAP Mill Products Industry Solution. Until her nomination as IBU director, she was a project manager in the metal and retail metal industry centre. She has worked at SAP AG since 1989 and has been involved in product development and management for important projects in Germany and abroad.

Dr Kerstin Geiger studied mechanical engineering at the University of Karlsruhe in Germany and received a doctoral degree in 1994. After her graduation, she worked for a German car manufacturer that led her to a year-long study of reverse engineering in Japan. She served as the overall coordinator for a study on new methods in product development for the German government. Starting in 1996, she worked for some time as an application consultant for product data management and product development in several projects in the high-tech and motor industries. She joined SAP AG in May 1997 and became responsible for product management for car manufacturers in the SAP Automotive IBU.

Prof Dr Henning Kagermann studied mathematics and physics in Brunswick and Munich (Germany). He received a doctorate in theoretical physics in 1975, and a professorship for physics and IT in 1980. In 1982, he began work at what was then SAP GmbH, where he was involved in the development of product areas for cost accounting and project controlling. He has served on the board of directors of SAP AG since 1991. His worldwide responsibilities include sales and distribution, consulting and customer relationships. He also approves business plans between regions and industries along with customer-specific development tasks relating to mySAP.com. He also holds responsibility for the development of the Industry Solutions for Banking, Insurance, Public Sector and Healthcare along with Strategic Enterprise Management (SEM) and Corporate Financial Management (CFM). Since 1998, Professor Kagermann has served as one of the two spokespersons for the board of directors and, as such, is responsible for the administration and financial areas of SAP AG.

Dr Gerhard Keller studied electrical engineering and business. He earned a doctorate in 1993 from the University of Saarland in Saarbrücken (Germany) with an emphasis on business. At that time he worked with various application-oriented research projects in the area of computer integrated manufacturing. In 1991, he led the development of methods for mapping business processes as part of a project for SAP AG. Dr Keller moved to SAP AG in 1992, where he was responsible for model architectures, particularly reference business processes. Since 1999, Dr Keller has been a member of the board of directors of bflow* AG, where he is responsible for the development of a virtual business network for supplemental SAP components. Under his direction, www.bflow.com is currently creating a global Internet portal for supplemental SAP solutions and announcements of SAP projects in which SAP customers, together with SAP software and consulting partners, can participate.

Markus Kerle studied business IT at the technical college of Karlsruhe, Germany, and has worked as an enterprise consultant since 1985 on international projects in the construction and motor industries. First as a developer and application consultant, and then as a project manager, he has focused on the development and implementation of standard software for internal company logistics and distribution. He has worked at SAP AG since November 1997 in the Automotive IBU. After 12 years as a consultant for clients in the motor industry in Asia and Europe, he has been the project manager for supply chain operations in the motor industry since July 1999.

Dr Holger Kisker worked at the Toyota Technological Institute in Nagoya, Japan, after receiving his doctorate. In 1996 he moved to SAP AG in Walldorf in Baden, Germany. He is now program director in the SAP Oil & Gas business areas, and holds responsibility for the contents and scheduled planning of the mySAP Oil & Gas Industry Solution.

Christa Koppe has worked at SAP AG since 1992. She has held various positions in sales, alliance management and marketing. Since October 1999, she has held responsibility for the Service Provider IBU, particularly for business development.

Dr Martin Przewloka is responsible for the worldwide product management of the SAP Service Provider solution in the Service Provider IBU. He also coordinates development activities of the Service Provider IBU.

Hans-Dieter Scheuermann, director of the SAP Insurance Industry Solution, studied mathematics at the University of Heidelberg in Germany from 1973 to 1978. Since then he has worked at SAP AG, first as a developer for financial systems (Financial Accounting, Controlling and Treasury). He then assumed responsibility for the coordination of international accounting systems. Between 1991 and 1998 he was the director of development for the R/2 and R/3 financial systems. He is the initiator of SAP software development for Public Sector and coordinates the mySAP Industry Solutions for banks, insurance and corporate treasury. He now has worldwide responsibility for GBU Financials.

Kay Smagowicz has a Master of Science in Administration degree from Boston University. She has been with SAP AG since 1998 working as a Product Specialist for the mySAP Financials Real Estate solution.

Daniel Stimson, Industry Marketing Manager, studied business at the University of South Carolina, USA, and in Vienna, Austria. He holds an MBA in international business. He worked for the computer industry in California for some time before moving to SAP marketing and pre-sales in 1996.

Jürgen Weiss studied business IT at the University of Heidelberg, Germany, after having trained as an editor; he then worked in publications at the Westdeutsche Landesbank in Düsseldorf. He has worked at SAP AG since, 1997 where he began in the Complementary Software Programme. He worked in the Regional Industry Group of the Insurance IBU, where he focused primarily on the new claims management sub-component, mySAP.com, and CRM activities for the Insurance IBU. He currently works as product manager in the GBU Financials.

Peter Wesche worked in retail for eight years after studying mathematics at university; in 1985, he turned to operations research and IT systems in retail. He has worked in logistics development at SAP since 1987; in 1992, he began the development of SAP Retail as project manager. He assumed responsibility for additional Industry Solutions within the supply chain in 1998.

Bodo Wielsch has a degree in business management and has worked at SAP AG since 1986. He began as a developer in the R/3 area, and then assumed responsibility for various Project System (PS) developments in the R/3 area. In addition to designing training courses, he has led various implementation projects for several customers in Germany, Switzerland, Austria, the Netherlands, South Africa, Australia and the USA. Since January 1998 he has worked as worldwide project manager for the Engineering & Construction area in the Aerospace & Defense/Engineering & Construction IBU. He is also the founder and chairperson of the European ETO Forum.

Gregor Wittreck studied business IT with an emphasis on process modelling at the University of Münster in Germany. Since 1995, he has worked as a consultant and project manager for international projects, primarily for chemical and pharmaceutical companies. His consulting activities focus on production logistics (R/3 PP and PP-PI) and supply chain management. He directs SCM/APO consulting at IMG AG.

Volker Zimmermann joined SAP's training department for accounting applications in 1991. In 1995 he managed the global rollout of SAP's R/3 Capital Investment Management functionality, positioning the newly created product internally as well as for customers and partners. In 1999, he was appointed Global Product Manager for SAP's Real Estate management solutions that are currently available as mySAP Financials Real Estate. He is responsible for globally marketing and positioning the product, and coordinating the partners' and customers' networks.

CHAPTER 1

The SAP Industry Strategy

Interview with Prof Dr Henning Kagermann

The development and rise of SAP AG as the largest worldwide manufacturer of software for enterprise resource planning (ERP) took place thanks to the company's founders and committed employees. Dr Henning Kagermann belongs to this group of formative employees. He joined the board of directors in 1991 and, along with co-founder Hasso Plattner, has served as its spokesperson since 1998. Kagermann initiated the industry orientation of SAP.

Dr Gerhard Keller conducted this interview with his co-author, Dr Kagermann. Keller possesses a thorough knowledge of SAP topics and helped conceive the *SAP Business Roadmap* series from SAP PRESS.

Keller SAP began a broadly-based structure for industry-oriented business units a good two years ago. Has the strategy of Industry Business Units so far proven correct?

The industry orientation of SAP

Kagermann Looking back, we made the right decision at the right time. Customers kept approaching us with their desire for solutions that responded to industry-specific requirements. The Oil & Gas and Healthcare Industry Solutions developed in 1991 gave us good foundational knowledge of how to convert these kinds of requirements into reality.

Keller Will SAP strengthen its industry orientation in the future?

Kagermann When I consider that today our 13 IBUs can offer tailor-made solutions to companies in 20 industries throughout the world, I see tremendous development performance in a relatively short time. We got to this point only because of close dialogue with our customers. We must and will continue the dialogue to have our solutions meet the requirements of specific industries. At the moment we're talking about further development; new Industry Solutions are not an immediate concern.

Keller SAP also offers industry solutions to mid-size companies. Do these offerings differ from the industry solutions for large companies?

Solutions for medium-sized companies

Kagermann We always design our solutions for an entire industry, regardless of a company's size or the specific segment of the industry in which it operates. In any case, the industry solutions can be tailored to a company's size. We offer SAP industry package and SAP.readytowork solutions especially for mid-size companies below a certain number of users and infrastructure.

SAP.readytowork

To complement the industry solutions of its individual IBUs, SAP has designed tailor-made, dedicated solutions for mid-size companies. These designs include industry package solutions, offered at a fixed price, and SAP.readytowork solutions. The former is designed for companies with 15–30 SAP users and annual revenues over $12.5 million. The latter addresses companies with 5–20 SAP users and annual revenues of $2.5 to $12.5 million.

The SAP.readytowork packages involve preconfigured industry solutions with a thin, industry-specific user interface. Examples here include the management of commercial real estate, retail management for building materials, information management for furniture retailers and special solutions for the food and meat industry.

The readytowork solutions contain default settings for all the essential functions that enable quick and easy use of SAP R/3. With the SAP.readytowork package, users receive a transparent solution offered at a fixed price, assurance of the ability to enhance the solution later, and a clear overview of the training required for individual business processes.

Keller What about diversified groups that operate in several industries?

Solutions for hybrid groups

Kagermann Such companies can also use several industry solutions. For example, Application Link Enabling (ALE) permits the combination of data for a consolidated corporate balance statement, the introduction of centralized purchasing or operation of group-wide cash management. Hybrid groups often feature cross-industry administration of common elements, such as personnel management and portions of financial accounting and controlling, in central areas. For easy identification of cross-industry functions, each of which can be used in various Industry Solutions, SAP offers a corporate function map.

Keller   How does SAP ensure that its Industry Solutions also consider the special features of various regions? The public sector works differently in Asia, the United States and Europe.

Country-specific special features

Kagermann   The Industry Business Units own their industry solutions; they coordinate the development of the Industry Solutions and second level support throughout the world. Country-specific development occurs in regional SAP development centres known as SAP Labs. To remain as close as possible to customers, both development and support follow the principles of decentralized organization.

   To remain with your example, it's important to speak the language of the customer. In fact, the public sector works differently in Asian countries than it does in Europe or North America. Nonetheless, functional commonalities exist in all sectors. For example, in all countries passports are requested from and issued by the competent authority, taxes paid or spent, construction permits are issued and budgets are prepared. This factor makes it sensible to run development threads together. Sales and distribution, consulting, training and linkage of local SAP partners, however, remain the responsibility of each country.

Keller   Companies collaborate not only within, but also across, industries. What does that mean in the context of mySAP.com with which SAP orients itself consistently toward the Internet?

mySAP.com

Kagermann   The Internet will develop into a dominant factor in economic life. Since it is a closely meshed network with multiple branches, it allows companies and their business activities to become networked together. In the past, companies placed orders by mail. Fax and electronic data interchange (EDI) have already enabled more rapid processing of this business transaction. Today, such transactions are processed in minutes over the Internet: ordering, order confirmation and invoicing. It makes no difference if the vendor is in Tokyo, Sydney, Paris, Buenos Aires or San Francisco. The relationships between companies are redesigned and exchange is accelerated: temporal and spatial distance have become almost meaningless.

   The same holds true for the creation, processing and availability of information. A global market demands global information. Business data must be up-to-date and globally available, all the time. Companies are not self-enclosed systems: they integrate with each other, and do so increasingly over the Internet. They are literally open on all sides, and only as such can they become part of the global economic network. That's the basic idea behind mySAP.com: to provide optimum support for business procedures and communication in an electronic age in a way that links internal and external applications and that considers all relevant security aspects.

Security on the Internet

The most widespread security mechanism on the Internet today is the secure sockets layer method, also called SSL encryption. A public key checks the identity of the participants, and both receive a procedure-specific key for the encryption of their communications. The procedure requires that the client and the server must have both a private key and a public key certificate (digital identity), issued by a certificate authority. Browsers contain preconfigured certificate lists from the certificate authorities. A certificate from an internal company certificate authority can identify its owner as an employee of the firm. The certificate can also include additional, person-specific characteristics, such as access authorizations.

To support virtual business, SAP security features include the following:

- The R/3 authorization concept, in which each system user has an authorization profile

- The security audit log, which continuously records security-relevant information and therefore has a deterrent effect

- The secure network communications (SNC) procedure to check the identity of communications partners and simultaneously encrypt the data flow

- The secure store and forward (SSF) method.

SSF protects R/3 data and documents when they are saved to disk and transmitted over potentially insecure communications channels. With SSF you can cloak R/3 application data and documents in secure, standard formats before transporting them electronically. During the process, digital signatures guarantee integrity (the data cannot be forged), authenticity (the signer can be uniquely identified) and proof of transmission and delivery (the creation of orders is verifiable). The digital cloak produced in the process ensures trustworthiness: only the intended recipient can view the data. Data protected with SSF remain protected even after the direct communications end and the data is stored.

Keller　Is mySAP.com a multifunctional platform?

Kagermann　mySAP.com is a multifunctional product because it always provides users with all SAP application components: R/3 modules, industry solutions and other components such as SAP Business Information Warehouse, mySAP Customer Relationship Management, mySAP Supply Chain Management, SAP Advanced Planner and Optimizer, and SAP Strategic Enterprise Management. mySAP always ships as a complete platform. Individual components have different release cycles, depending upon how quickly market demands change the components. The latest delivery of mySAP.com will always contain the most up-to-date development level of all components.

Keller　How will third-party products and external applications be integrated?

Integration

Kagermann   The integration occurs with BAPI technology and in the role-based mySAP Workplace. The Workplace functions as the front end of mySAP.com, the interface on the screen. The Workplace is not an application in itself. It's comparable to an individually-configurable Web browser. The Workplace can contain buttons that the user clicks to call or start specific functions. The Workplace consistently avoids depicting functional elements that the user does not need. The Workplace meets all of the requirements that were drawn up two years ago for EnjoySAP: to provide users with a user-friendly, clear and intuitive interface that makes work with our system an enjoyable experience.

Keller   You said that the Workplace was role-based. Would you explain that term with a concrete example?

The role concept

Kagermann   Every user of the Workplace plays one or more roles within their company: employee, purchasing agent, sales manager, production planner or controller.

The basic question asks what functions within the overall company system a specific user needs to play a specific role in the company. Does the purchasing agent need access to controlling components? Of course not. Does the production planner need the customer management system? Probably not. But both need data from SAP Materials Management to perform their work, and the Workplace allows both to access that data. In addition, the purchasing agent also needs SAP Business-to-Business Procurement and possibly even archiving software.

The purchasing agent will find these functions in the Workplace within the context of mySAP.com. The Workplace provides the purchasing agent with third-party products, such as e-mail or news programs, and self-configured mini-applications for reporting. The agent can set up the Workplace to include links to vendors, online services, airlines or hotels. The role of purchasing agent requires three of the software applications provided by SAP.

Keller   Yet the purchasing agent has much more available?

Kagermann   In principle, the agent can use functions from all components. But is that necessary? Let's use the example of an employee in the human resources department. While the employee essentially deals with the administration of other employees, the role changes if the employee is promoted to a management position. Here questions of personnel development and compensation take centre stage. The new requirements refine the role. For example, the newly promoted manger can remove functions that deal with the administrative processing of applications from mySAP Workplace.

Keller   Is the role of a purchasing agent the same everywhere, or does it depend upon the industry? There must be a difference between selling insurance and steel, or between preparing for work in a chemicals company or in the tool and die (mechanical engineering) industry.

mySAP Workplace

At first glance, mySAP Workplace is like a software interface for editing text, working with spread-sheets or creating a presentation: it is a window on a computer screen. But this comparison is not entirely accurate because the Workplace itself is not a business application: it allows access to business applications. Its appearance varies depending on the user. The Workplace interface for a purchasing agent looks different from that of a salesperson, a controller or a production plan-ner. For day-to-day work, the purchasing agent needs different functions from the controller, and configures the Workplace accordingly.

The buttons on the purchasing agent's screen can access the mySAP.com component for Materials Management (SAP MM), the SAP Business Information Warehouse (BW), SAP Business to Business Procurement (SAP BBP), the company's internal intranet, the online product catalogues of six vendors, current exchange rate data and the company's archive system, which may be provided by a third party. The purchasing agent can call each of these functions on the screen. As a user, the purchasing agent does not have to worry about what application (SAP MM, SAP BW or SAP BBP) applies in a specific case. The Workplace handles seamless interaction between the components: it posts the material order from the lowest-bidding US vendor at that day's exchange rate and stores it in the archive system.

Users only need to identify themselves once at the Workplace, and can then use all the appli-cations linked to the Workplace. From the Workplace, users have access any time and anywhere: from a laptop while on the road or over the intranet while on-site. Users can change the func-tion buttons on the Workplace as they wish.

Kagermann   Of course there are differences according to industry, which is why function-ally identical roles have different, industry-specific characteristics. Work preparation involves lists of chemicals in the chemicals industry and bills of materials in the tool and die industry. The description of roles in the mySAP Workplace takes this situation into con-sideration. By mid-year, mySAP.com will offer 142 cross-industry and 75 industry-specific roles.

Keller   What's the basis for pricing a user role? General availability or actual use?

Kagermann   Pricing is primarily oriented towards a user's role, regardless of how often the user activates the role.

Keller   Does the new role-based understanding of SAP supersede the modelling of business processes?

Role and business process

Kagermann   No. The definition of a user role complements the modelling of business processes. Modelling will certainly become more broad-based. In the future, modelling will map not only the business process of a specific company, but also include those of several companies. Modelling must reflect the increased networking in the business world by including interactive business processes.

Keller Won't the users' roles also change in time?

Kagermann The definition of specific roles will change. We will continually develop the roles functionally, and make the growing supply of roles available to our mySAP.com customers, analysts and partners. Interested parties can evaluate new roles in the Internet Demonstration and Evaluation System (IDES) on the Internet.

Keller Many employees with roles require formatted and informative data for their work. Can the Business Information Warehouse (SAP BW), which prepares such analyses, also handle the industry-specific need for information?

Business
Information
Warehouse

Kagermann Of course. To support industry-relevant processes with SAP BW, we are developing our new information model, the business context along with the Industry Business Units. For example, the IBU Retail model will contain a shopping basket analysis, IBU Pharmaceuticals will feature an index of market share, IBU Banking will provide data to analyse the risk of a portfolio, IBU Media will analyse advertising and IBU Automotive will enable just-in-time (JIT) evaluations.

Keller Simply by clicking with the mouse in the Workplace?

Kagermann SAP BW makes its information and analyses available throughout a company according to the principle of publish and subscribe. Every authorized user can request that data from the Workplace. In the context of mySAP.com, SAP Business Information Warehouse has new meaning. Because it also links data from external systems with internal company data, the BW has become a central solution for business intelligence and reporting.

Keller Give me a practical example.

Kagermann Consider the sales manager who wants to improve profitability in a specific region. To reach this goal, the manager must find answers to a series of questions. SAP Logistics will provide a good number of answers, but the manager also needs additional information such as sales costs from mySAP Financials, data on market potential from a market research company, or quality data from an external system. Only the integrated design of a data warehouse can combine such data and evaluate it across applications: just what the SAP Business Information Warehouse provides.

SAP Business Information Warehouse (SAP BW)

SAP Business Information Warehouse is much more than a business information system; it does much more than make information available. Developed on the basis of the business model, SAP BW works with specifically defined information models (business content) that users can modify to meet their own needs. From the sources available, such as R/3 data, it extracts data related to specific business processes, combines it and formats it for decision-support, reporting or analysis. SAP Business Information Warehouse makes information that is relevant to planning and decisions available throughout a company, at all levels of the company. It gathers individual solutions into a complete solution and integrates analysis results into operative business processes.

Keller   What does mySAP.com mean for the industry solutions?

Kagermann   Obviously, companies from various industries will also profit from the integrated functions of mySAP.com. They can combine the functions they need according to their requirements. Virtual teams, such as purchasing agents or production planners, can act across specific functions.

     The lines between companies, industries, sectors and markets are no longer drawn as clearly as they once were. Mergers, takeovers and inter-company cooperation dissolve and redraw the lines. This creates completely new business models in specific areas. The utilities industry is a good example of these developments, which also make new demands on business software systems. Such systems must offer users functional depth not only within the company, but functional breadth across companies. They must be able to link functions from external systems, such as supplier systems. mySAP.com flexibly fits companies as they change their frontiers.

Keller   mySAP Marketplace developed in the context of mySAP.com. Is a single marketplace enough in a global market, or will several industry-specific marketplaces develop?

mySAP
Marketplace

Kagermann   Under mySAP.com, SAP has built a functioning marketplace that it operates itself. The marketplace already includes more than 3,500 registered companies that trade with each other in various ways. By the end of March, more than 60,000 users had registered for mySAP Marketplace; we get over 1.2 million hits each day and the number is increasing. Additional marketplaces are being developed, such as the planned Telstra regional Marketplace for Australia and New Zealand.

     I am also convinced that sector marketplaces will succeed in the industry sectors. Our previous experience supports this conviction. In December 1999, SAP reached an agreement with worldwide chemical and pharmaceutical companies to establish an electronic marketplace.

Keller What will these sector marketplaces trade?

Sector
marketplaces

Kagermann So far, they have handled repair and maintenance for assets in the chemical and pharmaceutical industries. These companies can calculate how long it will take to repair a failure in a complex production procedure. The marketplace lets them quickly find a specialist who can solve the technical problem.

In principle, the chemical and pharmaceutical marketplace supports every form of electronic commerce, along with collaboration and information exchange between participants. It can also serve to regulate supply and demand in a special sub-area of a sector.

Keller Will large enterprises be the only ones present in electronic marketplaces?

Kagermann Not at all. Large companies collaborate with many mid-size companies who also participate in the marketplaces. Some marketplaces will be open to all participants, and others will follow a book club model, allowing access only to a limited number of registered participants. Electronic commerce provides access to the largest market in the world – the Internet – to small and mid-size companies.

Keller Will SAP provide only the infrastructure for its marketplaces, or will it operate them itself in some form?

The SAP
Marketplace
strategy

Kagermann We must identify three separate business models. I have already touched on the first model, operated by SAP itself as the mySAP Marketplace.

The second model involves joint venture marketplaces, operated jointly by SAP and one or more of its strategic partners.

In the third model, SAP only provides the technology that makes the platform available. Individual companies or groups of companies then direct and handle the content of this type of marketplace.

Keller Do customers and suppliers who use ERP (enterprise resource planning) software other than mySAP.com have access to the marketplaces? What about small firms, who don't find it worthwhile to run their own business-software systems?

Kagermann Every company has the technical capacity to present its goods or services in the marketplaces, regardless of the software they use. We will also create interfaces that enable communication between different systems. But companies must already have the basic functions required for electronic commerce, even something as simple as a shopping basket. They must also be able to process the incoming data automatically.

Keller What's the next step?

Kagermann   I think that the different types of marketplaces described above will join together. An almost infinite number of links will dovetail these marketplaces with each other. I am convinced that a sort of Federation of Marketplaces will come into being.

Just as several companies decide to cooperate in a value chain, a shift will occur in the marketplaces. Marketplaces will consolidate just as companies do, to create commercial volume and offer market services at good prices. Consolidation will aim at creating value for the marketplace, customers and companies.

ValueSAP: Creating Permanent Added Value

Particularly in periods of rapid change, companies must constantly evaluate their information technology and tailor it to changed market environments. An effective enterprise solution optimizes business processes. But are processes really optimal when a company is forced to implement change?

ValueSAP is based on the realization that an implementation project need not end with the productive start of a solution. ValueSAP aims at the continuous creation of added value in a company. The correct hardware and software solution is as significant as its continual optimization. ValueSAP divides the usage of a system into three phases: evaluation, implementation and continuous business improvement (CBI). During the entire life cycle of a company's system, each of the three phases employs methods, tools and content to identify the most important business processes and measure their value for the enterprise.

Industry-specific SAP solution maps and key performance indicators (KPI) are the centre of a value-added design. KPIs are used throughout the entire ValueSAP process. The KPIs used during evaluation can also be used in the implementation phase to ensure that all eyes remain focused on the goal. Solution maps describe the most important processes within a sector and the technologies and services needed to support the processes. For example, in the evaluation phase, KPIs help recognize the connections between business processes by clarifying dependencies and setting the goals for added value.

The continuous business improvement (CBI) phase supports companies by continually optimizing their systems. It evaluates enhancements, process improvements and systems. A company's management can use proven tools and procedures to analyse the current state of the enterprise, remind itself of its original goals, adjust the goals if necessary and identify new business opportunities. The CBI phase also uses industry-specific, standard key figures developed by SAP partners. Companies of any size can tailor the services of continuous business improvement to their needs.

mySAP Aerospace & Defense Industry Solution

Martin Elsner and Mario Burmeister, SAP Systems Integration AG

2.1 AN INDUSTRY WITH A FUTURE

Outlook

In a period when global companies characterize the world of economics, unlimited mobility plays a decisive role. Air transport, the fastest-growing transportation platform, occupies centre stage in this development. The current growth rate for passengers is increasing by between 5 and 7 per cent annually, a trend that will likely continue into the future. Experts agree that the number of passengers throughout the world will double by 2010, while the number in Europe will double within the next 15 years.

Demand

The American manufacturer Boeing expects a demand for 14,000 new jets in the next 20 years, and the European Airbus consortium anticipates a need for 13,400 aircraft in the same period. Both estimates rest upon the expected rate of growth for the world economy and the replacement of old planes. More than 80 per cent of aircraft currently in use must be replaced in the next two decades. The reasons are economic: as planes last longer, maintenance costs increase, and older planes burn unacceptable amounts of fuel. Fulfilment of the projected demand depends upon whether business for airlines develops as positively as forecasted.

2.1.1 Industry Diversification

Outsourcing

The time when one airline company could handle all business areas technically required for air transport, from ground service to flight connections, seems to be over. More and more airlines split off their technology into independent companies or simply sell them. Given the trend toward concentration on core competencies, a company will only hold on to those business areas that are economical in the long term. The aerospace industry has used diverse operations for some time (manufacturers and operators), but the trend toward outsourcing has accelerated diversification. Outsourcing also affects the need for various types of software. Despite diversification, all business areas in the world market operate under tremendous pressures to reduce costs.

Manufacturers

Civil aviation

This chapter only deals with companies that produce aircraft and engines as manufacturers. The manufacturer group is the smallest quantitative unit in the aerospace and defence industry. The group can be sub-divided into firms that produce civil (commercial) or military aircraft.

Although some manufacturers produce both kinds of aircraft, the following comments apply most specifically to civil aviation. For a long time, government subsidies coloured the market of aircraft manufacturers; success in the market depended upon political influences. Today, a few firms and quasi-governmental agencies dominate the market for large jets (those with 100 or more seats). A larger number of competitors produce aircraft with under 100 seats.

Capital-intensive development

A long and capital-intensive development phase, time-to-market, characterizes the manufacturing business. The products produced carry high prices, and are sold in relatively small numbers. Manufacturers must often work with customer-specific requirements.

Trends

Recently, manufacturers have become increasingly involved in the after-sales market. That area includes logistics; maintenance, repair and overhaul (MRO) services; leasing; and financing.

Suppliers

Safety standards

The supplier group in this section includes all vendors who manufacture components or assembly units for producing or reconditioning engines or aircraft. These products require a high degree of specialization, so usually only a few firms supply specific components. The firms must also deal with detailed requirements from supervisory authorities in each country to adhere to extremely high safety standards. The highly developed globalization of the supplier market partly results from the high degree of specialization among vendors.

Airlines

A fall in average
earnings

A steep decline in average earnings over the past years characterizes the highly competitive market among airlines. Airlines responded to this development with rigid cost management, which strengthened the trend toward concentration on core competencies. Accordingly, most airlines have already withdrawn from the MRO business. Although some airlines still perform their own maintenance, others have left this business area.

Global alliances

In addition, many airlines have formed global alliances. Some airlines still feed at the trough of subsidies, but others have positioned themselves very successfully in a market of free competitors. An important indicator for the economic success of an airline is its unit costs per mile, and the profit it earns, expressed in cents per mile.

Maintenance, Repair and Overhaul (MRO)

Globalization

Advanced globalization characterizes the MRO market. As a result, companies compete on the world market with extremely diverse pay scales. To an airline, it makes no difference if a D check (heavy maintenance) that lasts two to four months and costs several million dollars is performed in South-East Asia or North America. It has already amortized the additional flight time through low-percentage price differences. The hourly cost for extensive maintenance runs between $35 and $100 throughout the world. Companies in countries with high prices relocate simple and time-intensive work.

Joint ventures

MRO companies have developed an additional strategy to ensure their ability to compete: the formation of joint ventures in countries with low wages. For example, highly trained and therefore high-cost personnel are involved in important initial installation work, while joint ventures with low-wage countries handle less demanding tasks, such as heavy maintenance.

Capability

With this approach, MRO companies can continue to offer a wide range of services in the market, and can also perform their tasks economically. Nonetheless, MRO companies depend heavily on suppliers and manufacturers for spare parts. They must cover their requirements by turning to a traditional seller's market with high prices and long delivery times.

2.1.2 The Communications Structure in the Aerospace Industry

The Current Structure

Circular system

The communications structure in the aerospace industry is circular (*see* Fig. 2.1). The interfaces between the individual points are multifaceted, with little homogeneity. The procurement of spare parts often becomes a time-consuming communications process. Rarely does an airline or an MRO company not need a specific component immediately. The question then focuses on how much time the manufacturer needs to deliver the component.

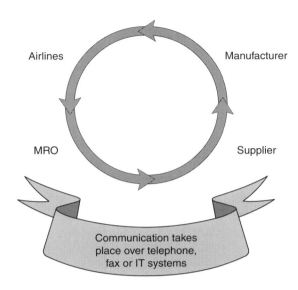

FIGURE 2.1 Communications in the airline industry today (©SAP AG)

Traditional
communications
methods

In the usual method, the airline or MRO requests the required component by telephone or fax from the manufacturer, who then orders the spare part from its supplier. In particularly rushed cases, a request might go out to a partner company to end the cost-intensive AOG (aircraft on ground) situation as quickly as possible. However, each of these steps costs time, and because of differences in time zones, it can well take days before locating and shipping the required part.

Communications in the Future

Internet

In the future, almost all communications in the aerospace industry will take place over the Internet. The world wide web enables rapid and standard communications, so that telephone, fax and 'snail' mail will retreat into the background. The hurdle to entry to the global market will become lower. New business opportunities will develop and lead to increased competition.

The aerospace industry may well work within the following scenario: an airline or an MRO company under contract to an airline requires a specific component (Fig. 2.2).

mySAP
Marketplace

The airline or MRO company uses the mySAP Marketplace to inquire after the component. One or more suppliers of the component have already registered the product on the Marketplace. The software generates a request to possible vendors. The supplying vendor can transfer the inquiry directly into SAP R/3, into the SAP Sales and Distribution (SAP SD) application component. The vendor's ERP system determines the planned lead time and costs (including profit margin). After successful processing, the

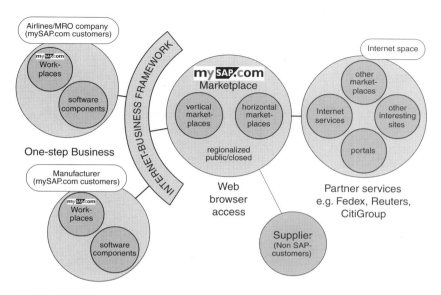

FIGURE 2.2   Future communications in the airline industry (©SAP AG)

supplier posts its quotation in the Marketplace. If the airline or MRO company accepts the quotation, the vendor's system automatically triggers production or assembly of the component or it triggers shipment of an in-stock component.

2.1.3 Prospects

Global competition challenges every aerospace company: the market environment is difficult and characterized by long product life cycles, decreasing customer loyalty, frequent restructuring and increasingly specialized customer requirements.

Continuous improvement of processes

Dynamic companies react to such a market environment by including new business areas, expanding their supply chains and shortening development time. To manufacture the best products at the best prices and at high quality, new technologies must support the changes required. The Internet is one of the new technologies that a global company simply cannot avoid.

Today most companies limit their involvement with the Internet to a presentation of the company and its products. The use of this medium will expand greatly in the near future. Most of today's Internet applications are linked to ERP systems and require double data entry, by the vendor and the purchaser.

The future belongs to systems that enable almost seamless connections between an Internet application and an ERP system, much as mySAP.com does. Seamless connections are an indispensable precondition for business-to-business and business-to-consumer commerce. The Internet also permits access to an ERP system from anywhere in the world, whether the user makes an inquiry or transmits information. It demands that a company expand its IT landscape.

Some 200 companies in the aerospace industry already work successfully with SAP R/3. Many companies in the MRO industry increasingly use SAP software.

Time-to-market life-cycle costs

Time-to-market and life-cycle costs are the key terms for success in the aerospace and defence industry. To meet these requirements, companies need a system infrastructure that can adjust to the rapidly changing business practices of manufacturers and implement improved developments. Companies must reduce costs while suppliers to the public sector must adhere to numerous standards for products, accounting and reporting. Against the background of these requirements, SAP R/3 links a complex series of business processes into a logical flow.

Industry-specific solution

With R/3 Release 3.0F, SAP offers industry-specific solutions for the special processes of the aerospace and defence industry. The solutions were developed in close collaboration with pilot customers from the aircraft maintenance, aircraft and aircraft component industries, along with regulatory agencies. To make the required processes as accessible as possible, the solutions include supplemental functions in the areas of quotation/invoicing, cost estimating, Cross Application Time Sheet (CATS), manufacturer part number, Spec2000 and progress. Many of the solutions have found a place in other industries. The engineering and construction industry and the automotive industry face similar problems. SAP has therefore adopted a strategy that includes all newly developed functions in the standard SAP R/3, as far as is reasonable and technically possible.

2.2.1 Aerospace and Defense Solution Map

The Aerospace and Defense Solution Map provides an overview of the critical process in the industry (*see* Table 2.1). This structured methodology identifies the industry-specific requirements from the process view and enables SAP R/3 to supply the information that companies need for success in the highly competitive market. For example, the Solution Map highlights some key processes that significantly influence the return on investment (ROI).

Project System: The kernel of the aerospace solution

The Solution Map illustrates the four industry groups. Manufacturers will recognize their critical processes primarily as develop to order, make to order and engineer to order; suppliers and MRO companies will find their processes are spares supply and maintenance repair and overhaul. Customer relationship management, enterprise management and business support are functions relevant to all companies. But an additional attribute characterizes all companies in this industry equally.

The SAP Project System (SAP PS) is the heart of SAP R/3 in the aerospace industry. It

TABLE 2.1   Aerospace and Defense Solution Map

Enterprise Management	Strategic Enterprise Management	Business Intelligence	Managerial Accounting	Financial Accounting			
Customer Relationship Management	Market Research & Analysis	Customer Service	Sales Management	Sales Cycle Management	Installation Management	Service Agreements	Service Fulfilment
Research & Development	Design, Concept & Specification	Quotation & Contract Costing	Order Entry	Engineering, Prototyping & Product Development	Hand Over and Contract Preparation		
Project Management, PDM/CM, Quality Management							
Make To Order	Inquiry & Quotation Processing	Order Entry Processing	Manufacturing, Assembly and Shipping	Preparation of In-service Support Data	Spare Parts Management	Warranty	
Project Management, PDM/CM, Quality Management							
Engineering To Order	Concept & Product Development	Inquiry & Quotation Processing	Order Entry Processing	Procurement, Shipping & Assembly	Start Up & Warranty		
Project Management, PDM/CM, Quality Management							
Maintenance, Repair & Overhaul	Sales & Marketing	Maintenance Engineering	Spares Management	Maintenance Planning	Work Planning & Preparation	Work Execution	Work Closure
Project Management							
Line Maintenance	Maintenance Engineering	Line Maintenance Control	Spares Management	Line Station Planning	Inspection	Execution	Completion
Airline Operations	Strategic Planning & Market Information	Sales & Service	Planning	Operations	Ground Services	Revenue Accounting	Route Profitability
Business Support	Human Resource Core Functions & Strategy	Human Resource Analytics & Enabling Solutions	Procurement	Treasury/ Corporate Finance Management	Fixed Asset Management		

helps combine the highly complex and correlative individual steps in production or maintenance into a clear, overall view. It assists the manufacturer with rough and detailed planning of individual steps in aircraft development, controlling costs and budgeting. It depicts production orders in a structure that enables properly scheduled pre-planning with the push of a button. The SAP Project System supports the maintenance business with scheduling functions for the creation of quotations and capacity planning. Settlement and invoicing orders are executed primarily in Project System (see the sample application in Section 2.3).

2.2.2 Sample Scenario

A process from maintenance can easily show the complexity of activities in this industry. In general, excellent technical support is the key to satisfied and loyal customers for companies providing services.

Sales and marketing

The mySAP Industry Solution for Aerospace and Defense (SAP A&D) offers a combination of tools to support the sales and marketing activities that precede the acquisition of a service product such as the C check for an aircraft. mySAP A&D provides functions to calculate quotations that you can compare to current prices on the market, and therefore estimate the potential profit. The quotation also serves as the basis for rough planning, capacity planning and the creation of customer contracts.

Condition and service data

Aircraft and engines must always remain in excellent condition and be safe to fly. To meet these needs, the SAP solution supports tracking of condition and service data, such as flight hours and number of landings, for each component of the aircraft. Based upon maintenance strategies, you can use this service data to schedule maintenance of the aircraft, engines and all other components.

Unplanned maintenance events

The Aerospace and Defense Solution can also handle unplanned maintenance events, such as those triggered by a pilot's request to perform an immediate repair at the next landing or maintenance interval. The structural models in the R/3 Project System can accurately schedule and perform even highly complex and involved maintenance and service activities such as D checks or engine overhauls. The structural models integrate materials, capacities and documents to guarantee maximum system support for maintenance.

Inspection and planned maintenance events

The system automatically creates and schedules planned orders, including the inspection of aircraft and activities mandated within a maintenance interval. A series of tools support aircraft inspection and generate the required work orders. Inspections often identify damaged parts; this discovery leads to unforeseen activities. The Project System can document and execute these findings.

Planning and scheduling

Based upon available work capacities, materials, spare parts and tools, the mySAP Industry Solution supports detailed planning and scheduling of the entire maintenance or overhaul project. The function for extended vendor provisioning supports the creation of work orders performed by subcontractors. The most expensive parts of an aircraft are usually repaired, rather than simply replaced, as is often the case in the automotive industry. The legal requirements for documentation mean that the system must be able to give an accurate depiction of the maintained structure, defined as the measures taken and the current configuration of the aircraft. The SAP solution provides a series of tools and functions here. For example, order status control ensures that all measures have been completed before you can begin subsequent activities.

Billing

Billing a maintenance project in the aerospace industry, particularly for government orders, is linked to many conditions. You must consider conditions negotiated in the contract and the costs of work orders. Expense-related billing in the A&D Solution automatically considers all the costs for labour, materials, tools and overheads. It generates invoices based upon the contract.

Documentation

Because the documentation of activities and measures plays an extremely important role in the industry, the A&D Solution collects data from the entire project in technical reports that you can supply to customers after completion of the order.

2.2.3 Development of the Business Solutions

Release 4.6 – enhancements

In R/3 Release 4.6, SAP now offers manufacturers in the aerospace industry a series of solutions for industry-specific issues. The solutions include the manufacturer part number, developed in collaboration with SAP Systems Integration AG in a customer project. SAP also provides solutions for serial number validity and Spec2000 processing. Enhanced processing for stock provided to a vendor and an improved design for counter reading are currently in development.

Development for airlines and the MRO sector

The solution will also include significant functional enhancements for airlines and the MRO sector:

▩ Maintenance Workbench

▩ Inspection Workbench

These tools will simplify employees' ability to deal with order, time and material confirmations on the shop floor. Both solutions are currently being developed in the context of a customer project and will be integrated in mySAP A&D when completed. As described in the sample scenario above, the configuration of an aircraft has enormous significance. The configuration management of aircraft is a particularly important function for airlines. It enables comparison of the current configuration of an aircraft to the permitted configuration given in the illustrated parts catalogue (IPC). Customers can quickly and reliably decide if a different configuration has cost benefits.

Optimization instead of automation

The development of ERP software has undergone a clear shift in the goals and requirements of a system solution. The primary goal in the past aimed at optimization of processes within the company, or best practice business processes. Today, however, there is a sharper focus on cross-company elements, and the supply chain occupies the foreground. Companies are no longer concerned only with the automation of their own processes. They regard it as much more important to optimize the entire value-added chain beyond the limits of a specific company. As an aid to performing this task,

SAP has developed products such as SAP Advanced Planner and Optimizer (SAP APO) and the Business Information Warehouse (BW). A consideration of SAP Advanced Planner and Optimizer can clarify the benefits.

SAP APO

SAP APO allows a company to link customers and vendors into its system-side processes and to coordinate processes with these partners. SAP APO includes supporting functions such as Supply Network Planning, which plans and optimizes capacity and material needs across companies, and Collaborative Planning, which enables planning of requirements together with vendors or customers. Requirements planning for a material no longer occurs within a plant; planning for a product or product group occurs globally together with the components. These functions contribute to closer networking between dependent partners and increase the efficiency of the participating companies (Fig. 2.3).

Is that the last step? Particularly in the highly competitive aerospace industry, characterized by mergers and takeovers, customer orientation and flexibility are now more important than ever. Against this background, mySAP.com provides an increasingly important building block for the future.

mySAP.com and Internet Marketplaces

Products in the aviation industry are of high quality and undergo several repair cycles before being scrapped. mySAP Marketplace opens a huge potential for cost savings here. Companies can use the SAP-directed Marketplace to offer their products to a

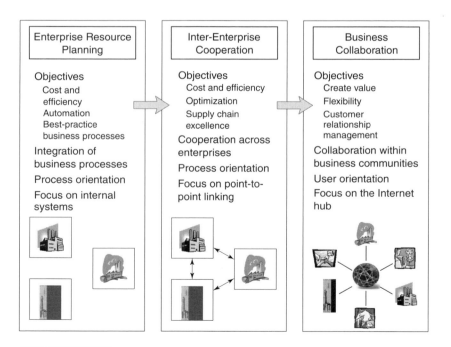

FIGURE 2.3   Development of the business solution (© SAP AG)

large group of customers or purchase materials and labour at good prices. Companies can also conduct auctions on the Internet Marketplace, offering their products for sale during a specific period and having purchasers bid on them. Sellers determine which offer to accept when the auction closes.

A company with a strong place in the market can also become the owner of its own marketplace on the Internet to optimize its own procurement process and sales activities. A joint venture marketplace, set up by SAP and a number of companies, offers yet another alternative. Companies run the common marketplace under their own names and SAP handles the technical background. For all non-SAP marketplaces, SAP offers application and base system infrastructure and can secure almost seamless integration with a company's ERP system (Fig. 2.4).

All the Marketplace platforms offer opportunities for use beyond buying and selling products over the Internet (e-commerce). Linking e-commerce, communities and information flow creates new possibilities for business collaboration.

mySAP.com and the web-based Workplace

The Solution Map clarifies the process-oriented use of SAP R/3. Future enhancements to the Solution Map include the user view, according to the roles played by specific users within a business scenario. mySAP Workplace, a web-based interface for a user's workstation, provides employees with access to all the system functions needed to fulfil their roles in the company. The functions can include processes both within SAP R/3 and over the Internet. mySAP.com combines both process elements and the role-based view in a highly flexible system that significantly shortens internal and external communications paths.

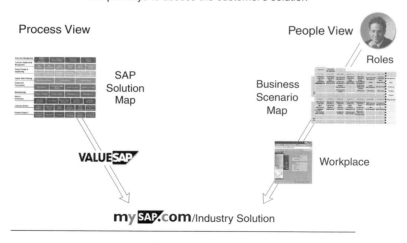

FIGURE 2.4   Connection between the process view and the role of a Workplace
(© SAP AG)

2.3 SAMPLE APPLICATION FROM A PROJECT OF SAP SYSTEMS INTEGRATION AG

Develop-to-order

Make-to-order

The following sketches an application scenario that maps the processes of an aircraft manufacturer, from development to make-to-order production. The two processes can be summarized as the process that develops the aircraft (develop-to-order, DTO), and the production process (make-to-order, MTO). The following example discusses the MTO process in greater detail.

During the DTO process, SAP Project System (SAP PS) supports development of the aircraft in an innovation project. The master data created and released during the process become the basis for production in the MTO process. Examples of the DTO process include development of prototypes in the aerospace or automobile industry and basic research or tool development in mechanical engineering.

The typical MTO process appears as follows. Based upon bid invitations or requests for quotations, a company creates a project in PS and uses SAP Sales and Distribution (SD) to assign the project to the appropriate account. The SAP PS application component supports customer-specific engineering activities. SAP PS also triggers external procurement (in SAP Materials Management, SAP MM) and internal procurement (in SAP Production Planning, SAP PP). The function for 'delivery from the project' (SAP PS) processes deliveries and shipping. Invoicing occurs according to an invoicing schedule triggered by PS. The SAP Controlling (SAP CO) application component, supported by SAP PS, controls costs and revenues.

For example, a customer might need a quotation for an aircraft. To estimate the quotation, the following tasks are processed:

- Creation of a project (without network)
- Costing of the quotation (manual level of the work breakdown structure)
- Rough scheduling (manual level of the work breakdown structure)

Inquiry/creation of a quotation

Once processing is complete, the customer receives the quotation. If an order results from the quotation, once both parties have agreed on the price and delivery date, the following process chain occurs.

The order is created in SAP SD. SAP PS generates a project from the data in SAP SD via assembly processing. The SAP PS application component stores the information needed to generate an operative project as a standard project (template). SAP PS then determines all the data required to flow into detailed costing or planning.

Lead times

The network maintains lead times for each activity. Relationships link (network) activities. For example, you can regulate a relationship between the procurement and assembly activities so that assembly begins two days after procurement ends. Backwards scheduling, which starts from the delivery date requested by the customer, determines the starting date. If the starting date is in the future, you can meet the delivery date requested by the customer.

Capacity
requirements

The function for capacity analysis identifies capacity bottlenecks such as personnel and machines. You can assign capacities and the required material components to each activity.

Costing

Cost calculation considers the costs for internal activities, primary costs, material costs and, if specified in a costing profile, overhead costs. Depending upon the schedule of the network, you can view the distribution of costs by period in the Information System. Scheduling considers the time for internal and external procurement.

BOM-PS interface

The BOM-PS interface simplifies the assignment of material components from one or more bills of material (BOMs) to network activities. The interface is used here to process BOMs and networks separately, but to keep the assignments up-to-date. The interface is particularly useful for engineering projects with continually growing construction BOMs.

PDM

This chapter does not describe product data management within SAP R/3. Those processes cover a series of software tools used for product-related information (BOM validity) and processes required for the design, manufacture (or assembly), and maintenance of products during the entire life cycle.

Implementation

After maintenance of the basic data, the implementation phase begins. The first step releases the required activities. Doing so triggers the transmission of requirements (pre-planning in SAP PS) to SAP PP for internal procurement and SAP MM for external procurement. The system then generates a purchase requisition or a planned order generated by a run of material requirements planning (MRP). The system transfers delays in the network to the purchase requisition or the planned order until they successfully convert into an order or a production order.

Implementation also includes consideration of the following points. SAP Project System confirms actual dates and actual hours to the activities. Doing so frees the cost centres, and charges the project with actual costs. This procedure integrates several application components: SAP CO, SAP FI, SAP PP and SAP MM. SAP PS functions much like a filing system to give you a clear overview of these complex procedures. You can also use SAP PS to trigger delivery after manufacture and an invoice once the project reaches invoicing milestones, and includes an invoicing plan.

Earned value

As work progresses, you can regularly control its earned value (EAV) by using the various reporting options in PS control schedules. For example, SAP PS automatically determines prognosis dates in addition to comparing planned and actual costs. You can use this information to see how delays affect the forecasted completion dates. You can also analyse milestones.

Confirming
activities

You enter dates in two ways. You can schedule manually for dates in the work breakdown structure, or use confirmed activities to determine the dates by extrapolating dates from the activities associated with dates in the work breakdown structure. The individual confirmations can be combined to form collective confirmations. You can also use functions for individual confirmation, Cross Application Time Sheets (CATS), or a decentralized plant data collection system. Confirmation of requirements cannot take place unless you have already released them manually or automatically (with release milestones). Release provides the preconditions for assigning costs to a project.

Actual costs in PS arise from activity allocation, confirmation, transfer posting and determination of overhead costs. Confirmations document the processing level of activities and activity elements. They offer a prognosis for further development.

Actual costs

The system automatically executes various functions, based upon the confirmations. These functions include posting actual costs, dates and labour and, if required, changing the status of an activity. In addition to simple comparisons of planned and actual costs, cost controlling can also consider budget constraints.

Milestones

The term 'milestone' needs some explanation here. Milestones are events that have a particular significance for a project. You can assign milestones to activities or elements of a work breakdown structure. For milestones used repeatedly in a project, you can set up standard milestones as templates.

In general, you can use milestones for the following tasks and functions:

- To trigger hard-coded functions in activities when milestones are reached
- To use milestones in earned value analysis
- To set dates in a customer order
- To gather information

As shown in Fig. 2.5, integration with SAP FI/CO (Financials and Controlling) plays an important role both during and after a project. The advantages of the SAP solution are clear: it integrates the classic functions of ERP software with the future-oriented possibilities of the Internet. SAP works closely with its customers to develop the software on an ongoing basis.

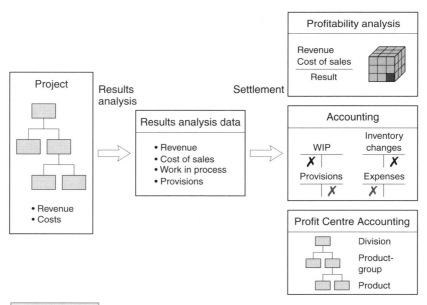

FIGURE 2.5   Integration of results analysis between PS/CO (© SAP AG)

mySAP Automotive Industry Solution

Dr Kerstin Geiger and Markus Kerle, SAP AG

3.1 THE AUTOMOTIVE INDUSTRY PREPARES FOR THE TWENTY-FIRST CENTURY

Markets

The automotive industry can look back at a century of successful and sustained growth. Two factors have led to the success of this industry. The human desire for mobility is one factor. The second factor arises from the flexibility of the automotive industry itself: it always reacted to the growing demands of its customers and changing markets. Interestingly, new legal requirements have triggered some trends in automotive technology, including regulations on emissions and safety. Growing environmental awareness has also played a significant role. The catalytic converter, the airbag and increased fuel efficiency are all innovations initiated from outside the industry. Automobiles are extremely common today, particularly in industrialized countries. In Western Europe more than half of the population owns a car; this figure increases to two-thirds in the US. It's no wonder then, that despite outstanding revenues in 1998 and 1999, automobile manufacturers speak of a saturated market and destructive competition. Forecasts see growth only for Eastern Europe, Asia (outside Japan), and Latin America (Selzle 6/99).

Heightened competition forces companies to react more quickly and more specifically to the individual desires of their customers in order to retain them as long as possible. To react both regionally and individually, the high-grade networked system of automotive manufacturers, system and part suppliers, development partners and sales partners must be organized and optimized globally (*see* Fig. 3.1).

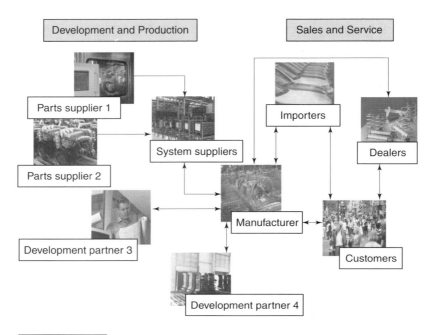

| Development and Production | | Sales and Service |

Parts supplier 1

Parts supplier 2

System suppliers

Importers

Dealers

Development partner 3

Manufacturer

Customers

Development partner 4

FIGURE 3.1   Networked business processes in the automotive industry (© SAP AG)

3.1.1 Globalization and Consolidation

Trends

Advances in IT increasingly enable companies to act globally. To cover regional and multi-regional needs as quickly and efficiently as possible, production sites and sales centres throughout the world have sprung up from the foundation of a group of affiliated companies. Prompt and reliable fulfilment of customer orders has become increasingly important. Whether ordering from a dealer or over the Internet, customers want to configure their cars individually and receive pricing and delivery information immediately. Automotive manufacturers strive to meet a time-to-customer delivery period (including order, production and final shipment) of five to ten days. Delivery time currently lies between two to eight weeks.

One of the most significant developments of the past few years in the automotive industry has been the mergers between automotive companies. On the manufacturing side, a few auto giants have arisen, who carried out strategic mergers or takeovers to offer a complete spectrum of products, from subcompacts to luxury vehicles. Consider the mergers between Daimler-Benz and Chrysler, between Ford and Volvo, or the structure of the Volkswagen group that today offers products in nine different markets.

This trend seems unbroken, and includes automotive vendors: TRW/LUCAS, Allied Signal/Honeywell and Bosch/Magneti Marelli. Experts predict further mergers in the next decade so that the year 2010 will see nine automotive producers instead of the twenty-one that exist today (Rhys 1999).

The background for this consolidation arises from insufficient revenues in the midst of satisfactory sales. Mergers allow companies to offer a balanced and complete selection of products. The effects of synergy through sales, development, production and distribution then allows them to bring the products quickly to market at good prices.

To meet its goals, the industry uses a platform strategy based on the use of equivalent parts that allows for the highest possible level of diversification among vehicles. The strategy even allows companies to bring niche vehicles to market at good prices and in acceptable timescales. In 1990 vehicles were produced on 174 platforms; within five years this number had decreased to 166. In 2000, only 123 platforms existed worldwide (Selzle 6/99).

The production depth and development activities of automotive manufacturers seem to tend toward the reverse proportion of the breadth of their product range. Today, 60 to 80 per cent of automobile development takes place externally. Manufacturers transfer more and more innovation and system responsibility for complete components to their suppliers, while keeping the number of direct suppliers as small as possible. For example, Ford has only 100 direct suppliers (Selzle 4/99). Manufacturers also delegate the task of managing subcontractors to direct suppliers. The distribution of tasks to a large number of participants makes the processes involved more complex because they run outside the borders of individual companies and require precise coordination and synchronization. This situation places enormous demands on a company's organization and IT systems.

3.1.2 Supply Chain Management

Trends

The supply chain in the automotive industry includes all the steps that add value, starting with raw materials and ending with a finished vehicle. Externally, the partners in the chain are heterogeneous. They include:

- System suppliers, who build complex products such as motors or high tech brake systems

- Component manufacturers, who supply finished and ready-to-install assemblies

- Parts manufacturers, who specialize in one production process

The size of the companies involved also varies considerably. The supply chain includes large companies with thousands of employees and diverse product lines as well as small firms that produce a single part.

The requirements for IT support of the processes involved varies just as widely. The development and planning forecasts of automotive manufacturers often directly involve system suppliers through collaborative planning and collaborative engineering.

Such collaboration requires a very close partnership with optimal communications. Partners share construction and planning information long before production actually begins. The process also includes several levels of suppliers.

Although no one disputes the desirability of comprehensive planning and optimization across the supply chain, the reality looks somewhat different today. Each partner optimizes their own processes in purchasing, inventory management and distribution. Manufacturers give their suppliers exacting requirements without considering the suppliers' planning. Planning and optimization across several levels seems almost impossible because systems, procedures and results are incompatible. A supply chain management system that includes all partners in planning, optimization and operative business is absolutely essential for the globalization of the market and supplier relationships of a future-oriented IT world (Fig. 3.2). New media and interfaces will render boundaries between companies and systems meaningless.

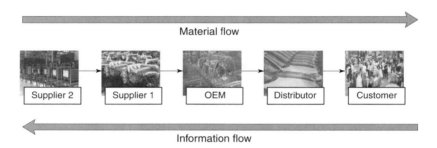

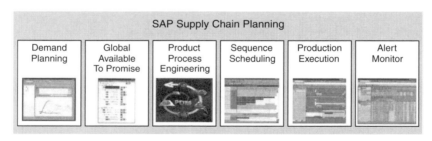

FIGURE 3.2   Optimization of the supply chain beyond company boundaries (© SAP AG)

3.1.3 Sales and Service

Trends

Vehicle sales and service has seen developments as dramatic as those in production. Some examples include direct sales, thinning out of dealer networks along with restructuring into pure service networks, and constant change in the sales strategies of manufacturers. The structure of global sales organizations has become more homogeneous; processes have been simplified and optimized. High costs continue to pose a problem, as does order-neutral production. Europe today still produces some two-thirds of all vehicles to 'stockpile' them, although manufacturers have set the goal of producing and delivering vehicles according only to customer wishes in the future. This approach would minimize costs, delivery times and high inventories.

Driven by increasing battles in markets that are becoming smaller while production capacity continues to rise, manufacturers have discovered an orientation to the customer that admits no compromise. Advertising, marketing, customer retention and advice, service and support are the current buzzwords. The industry must win new customers and simultaneously retain existing customers. These goals result in a completely new need for information, a need that goes well beyond that required in normal business. To survive, companies need business intelligence, complete knowledge of the market, partners, competitors and customers (*see* Fig. 3.3).

In response to these issues, software companies offer customers relationship management systems and information warehouses. As information procurement and analysis grows, so too does the need to let the results derived flow directly into planning and execution. This need requires the integration of production and information logistics, requirements met in mySAP.com.

For many partners in the dealer network, service will provide the business basis for the future. Today, hardly a single car dealer makes money selling new cars: profit margins are becoming smaller and generous discounts eat up whatever profits might be left. The dealers of the future will limit themselves to the delivery of new vehicles. Sales will come from central sales units or directly from the manufacturer. Today's dealers are the service stations of the future. Yet the service business also needs a lot of information

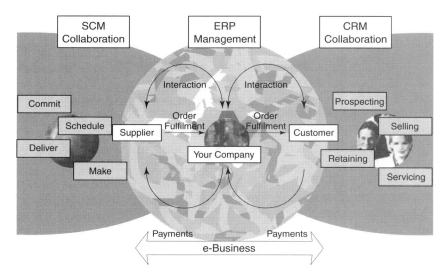

FIGURE 3.3   Customer Relationship Management and Supply Chain Management
(© SAP AG)

about spare parts or service that must be available to even the smallest operating units. The need for a simple, cost-effective, broadly available IT infrastructure is obvious, and the Internet offers the foundation for future solutions.

3.1.4 The Automotive Industry on the Internet

Various branches of the automobile industry use the Internet. The processes it supports are as varied as demands placed on any IT system: functions, user interface, ease of use and performance.

Fig. 3.4 illustrates sample scenarios:

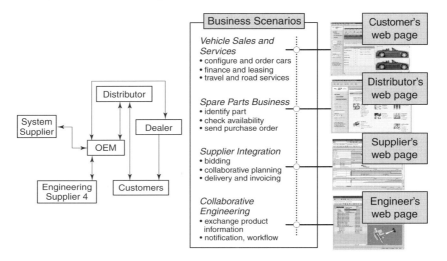

FIGURE 3.4   Business scenarios on the Internet (© SAP AG)

▓ **Customer**

An automobile customer orders their sports car on their home PC. They have all the information they need about equipment options. If they want to, they can see the price, delivery time and contract details for the options they like. They can then order the car with a click of their mouse.

▓ **Marketplace**

Manufacturers and suppliers post their inquiries and quotations on a common marketplace on the Internet. The Internet serves as a central communications medium to handle contract closing and settlement.

▓ **Purchasing Planner**

Purchasing planners see an up-to-date overview of all the materials for which they are responsible. Proactive alert monitors inform them of any exceptional situations.

They can see the overall situation at a glance, and can intervene at the right place with a few mouse clicks.

▪ **Managing Director**

The managing director of an automotive supply company receives a daily overview of the most important indicators from his company's own system and those of their partners on their computer screen.

The Internet and intranets provide the customer, supplier, purchasing planner and managing director with important information from various systems. A user has access to specific applications based upon their role in the business procedure.

| 3.2 | **THE SOLUTION FOR THE AUTOMOTIVE INDUSTRY** |

Integrated solutions

Leading manufacturers in the automotive industry have used SAP R/3 for several years to support business processes in the areas of human resources, financial accounting and logistics. To better address the needs of the industry, SAP began to develop the Automotive Industry Solution in 1997. Like the other Industry Solutions, mySAP Automotive uses the broad range of functions in mySAP.com. It also offers function-specific enhancements for the automotive industry. The add-ons offer targeted support for the complexity and extensive number of variants in automotive products. They enable better planning and processing of high-volume orders in the context of time-critical factors and numerous suppliers.

Development of industry-specific functional enhancements occurs only in close collaboration with SAP customers. Various reviews, defined as real-life functional tests, performed by a broad group of customers, ensure the usability of the solutions developed.

The first industry solution, mySAP Automotive 1.0, was successfully implemented in February 1999 with R/3 Release 4.0B. Suppliers and manufacturers with low order volumes (truck assembly) mainly use this version. SAP delivered mySAP Automotive 2.0, based upon R/3 Release 4.6B, in April 2000. By working with Release 3.0 of SAP Advanced Planner and Optimizer, mySAP Automotive Release 2.0 offers a functional scope that satisfies the demands of manufacturers with high order volumes.

The following Solution Maps provide an overview of the functional scope available in mySAP Automotive.

Workplace

mySAP Automotive 2.0 now includes workplaces typical of the industry. The workplaces provide employees with all the functions they need to perform their roles in the company. It includes workplace templates for management, persons responsible for specific areas and general roles. The mySAP Workplaces that appear on users' screens access not only SAP software, but also applications from other manufacturers and Internet services (stock market information, e-mail and search engines).

Preconfigured solutions

Since the introduction of mySAP Automotive Release 1.0, SAP has offered a preconfigured Industry Solution that simplifies implementation of the SAP system for small and medium-size companies. The preconfigured solution contains ready-to-use processes relevant to an automotive manufacturer. It enables implementation in the shortest possible time and with minimum expense.

3.2.1 Solution Map for Automobile Manufacturers

The Solution Map (*see* Table 3.1) illustrates the business processes that mySAP Automotive can support.

mySAP Automotive Industry Solution offers a consistent and process-oriented solution for industry-independent business processes such as enterprise management, customer relationship management and business support. Enhancements cover the following automotive business processes specific to manufacturers:

- Engineering
- Supply chain management and monitoring
- Procurement
- Manufacturing
- Sales
- CKD (completely knocked-down kits)

Engineering

One of the main challenges of the automotive industry involves reduced development times. Only development activities that run in parallel and the efficient use of already available information and solutions can reach this goal.

To support highly integrated processes, the development of the Industry Solution included Integrated Product and Process Engineering, which enables product structure to be mapped and linked (*see* Fig. 3.5).

Integrated Product and Process Engineering enables the development of product information in a Product Variant Structure. Depending upon the progress of the development work, you can begin by creating functional structures that represent the basic components of a product (vehicle with motor, transmission, body and so on). Little by little you can assign various documents or variants that describe the product more precisely.

You use the same procedure to map work schedules and assembly lines in the plant layout. You can create structures for work schedules and production lines to complete step by step. You can also set technical sequences for production tasks: for example, the 'attach' activity can only occur after the 'adjust steering wheel' activity has been completed.

You can assign product components to work schedules and work schedules to production lines at any time and with different levels of detail. The assignments form the basis for the optimization of assigning operations to cycle areas, the generation of product costs and the determination of part supplies for production.

With Integrated Product and Process Engineering, you can set views for the product

TABLE 3.1   Automotive OEM: Solution Map

	Strategic Enterprise Management	Business Intelligence	Managerial Accounting	Financial Accounting	Sales Cycle Management	Sales Channels	Installation Management
Enterprise Management							
Customer Relationship Management	Market Research & Analysis	Product/Brand Marketing	Marketing Programme Management	Sales Management			Installation Management
Engineering OEM	Engineering Projects	Product Engineering	Process Engineering	Target Costing	Product Data Management		
Supply Chain Planning & Monitoring OEM	Variant Demand Management	Resource Planning	Order Scheduling & Sequencing	Distribution Planning	Supply Chain Monitoring	Supplier Workplace	
Procurement OEM	Strategic Purchasing	Operative Procurement	Inbound Logistics	Inventory Management	Billing	Vendor Performance	
Manufacturing OEM	Supply to Line	Manufacturing Execution	Quality Management	Manufacturing Confirmation & Monitoring			
Sales OEM	Sales Planning	Direct Sales	Sales Execution	Vehicle Distribution	Billing	After-Sales Tracking	
Completely Knocked-Down Kits (CKD)	Planning	Packing & Shipping	Kit Management	Assembly	Manufacturing Confirmation & Monitoring		
Business Support	Human Resource Core Functions & Strategy	Human Resource Analytics & Enabling Solutions	Procurement	Treasury/Corporate Finance Management	Fixed Asset Management		

and process model, and supply the user with the relevant information. It also supports company-wide visualization of two- and three-dimensional geometry. You can also integrate CAD (computer-aided design) systems.

The integration with mySAP PLM (Product Lifecycle Management) provides you with change, document and configuration management.

The automotive industry usually produces vehicles in several plants on cycled assembly lines. Significant variations can arise between the load on production sites, the need for spare parts and the work performed on individual lines – independently of the level of orders or the configuration of individual vehicles.

Across several production sites and suppliers, the task of supply chain management is to guarantee both long-term programme planning and medium- and short-term planning of sequential orders while considering the goals of the business. Goals include:

▨ Equal loads for production sites and lines

▨ Minimized time to customer

▨ Minimized deviations from the absolute schedule

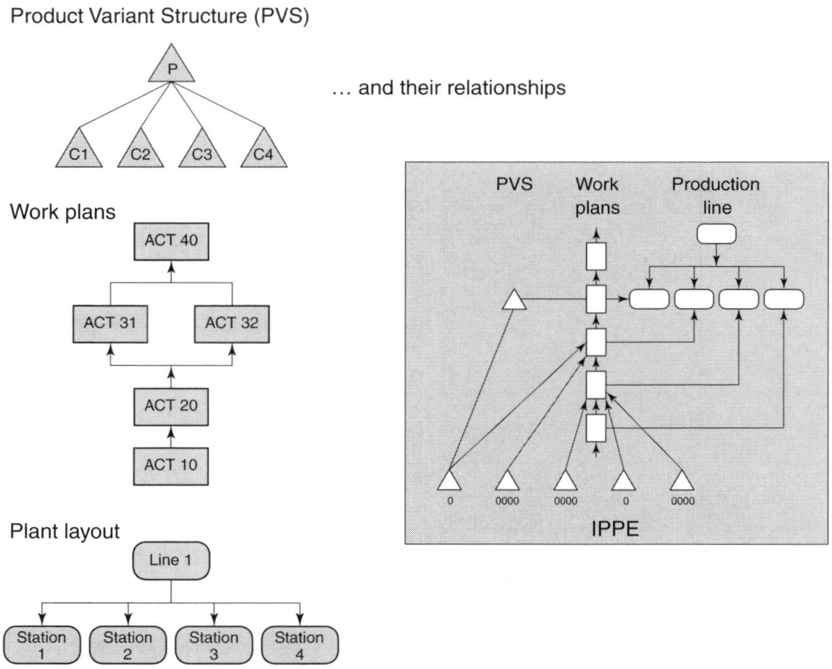

FIGURE 3.5 Integrated Product and Process Engineering in mySAP Automotive
(© SAP AG)

Within mySAP SCM (Supply Chain Management), SAP Advanced Planner and Optimizer (SAP APO) supports these tasks. SAP APO offers functions for planning, optimizing, executing and monitoring supply chains.

Special enhancements in SAP APO offer model mix planning that determines optimal order sequence with start and end dates.

Depending upon the planning period, you can divide the planning of the order sequence into two areas:

■ Period slicing for tactical planning in a planning window of several days or weeks before production. It assigns orders to assembly lines while considering quantity restrictions.

■ Sequence planning for operative planning in a planning window of a few hours or days before production. Sequence planning can consider various restrictions. It determines the optimal order sequence with a genetic algorithm and consideration of the business goals.

Fig. 3.6 illustrates the results of model mix planning. The screen displays the sequence plan for the production days and shifts depicted on the left. The status notifications `fixed` and `released` indicate the processing level of the orders. The screen displays

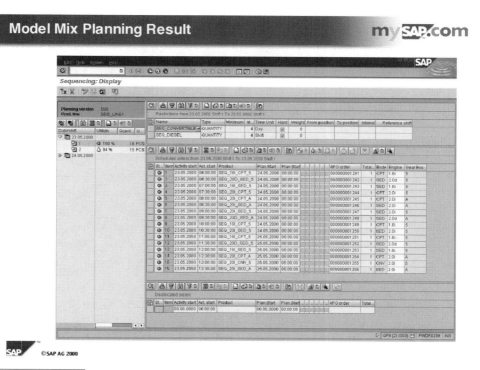

FIGURE 3.6   Results of model mix planning (© SAP AG)

any restrictions that apply to this shift above the sequence plan. Below the sequence plan, it lists unplanned orders that the purchasing planner can schedule using the 'drag and drop' method.

The rapid planning matrix provides the basis for requirements planning. It explodes BOMs of products with several variants and large order volume in a server's liveCache. The planning matrix sets the relationship between the maximum characteristics of the product (all the possible components of a vehicle) and the assembly orders, and lists the components to be built. The liveCache technology can execute requirements and range-of-coverage calculations in a few minutes. It can also generate scheduling agreement releases and pull lists and redirect them within the supply chain. The resulting flexibility not only provides manufacturers with some slack for optimization in the production process, but also enables them to react quickly to any breakdowns (such as delivery problems) in the supply chain.

Procurement

Purchasing and procurement of components includes several areas:

Strategic purchasing

Strategic purchasing selects vendors based upon various evaluation criteria. It can also manage complex contract, price, delivery and payment conditions for various plants. It can also map suppliers and parts catalogues as a basis for selecting components.

Operative procurement

In the automotive industry, the production of components that have a high value-added level is usually synchronized with suppliers. This is known as just-in-time (JIT) procurement. The suppliers base their requirements planning on the numbers and schedules transmitted by the manufacturers on a regular basis. Manufacturers can also transmit a JIT delivery schedule tailored to a specific day.

Logistics for goods receipt

mySAP Automotive can define regular routes for the goods receipt of components. It can also use shipping notifications from the supplier to track goods. The route enables manufacturers to define in detail how and when the material flows. In the case of a two-level goods receipt, the receiving office first compares the delivery papers with the previously transmitted data, and registers the arrival of the truck. A second level compares the inventory and value of the delivery with the expected inventory and value.

Manufacturing

After they have been fixed and released, assembly orders are executed, confirmed and settled at the appropriate lines. Seamless materials staging at lines in the automotive industry is extremely important: losses incurred because of a stopped assembly line are rarely recovered.

To improve the flow of information between manufacturers and suppliers, mySAP Automotive offers a Supplier Workplace. It enables suppliers to use a simple Internet browser for direct access to the manufacturer's system to track their own releases, deliveries and settlements. Forecast delivery schedule, JIT delivery schedules and summarized JITs can, of course, also be transferred by electronic data interchange (EDI).

For replenishment processing within and outside a company, mySAP Automotive offers KANBAN procedures and interactive materials staging lists.

To monitor assembly and work-in-process (WIP), you can assign a reporting point to the line. When the number of components reaches the point you have defined, the system automatically takes the correct quantity from stock and updates financial accounting with the appropriate positive and negative values. The use of liveCache technology is particularly well suited to this because it processes large order volumes.

Sales

mySAP Automotive also supports the complete planning process for vehicle sales. You can create sales forecasts as well as define and track dealer quotas, as well as create multilevel vehicle hierarchies that you can easily configure. This capability enables you to map platform design that offers numerous options for individual configuration by customers. Configuration can occur over the Internet or on an independent sales system (laptop). mySAP Automotive works in the background to ensure that the selected configuration is permitted and automatically determines the correct price (see Section 3.2.3, Solution Map for Sales and Service). It confirms customer orders and then plans and monitors distribution after the vehicle has been produced.

CKD

In countries that require final assembly of vehicles on site, companies process completely knocked-down kits (CKD). mySAP Automotive supports the creation of CKD kits with CKD bills of material and consideration of special CKD packing regulations. After an availability check has been carried out for all the required components, the kits are packed and shipped according to parts or as complete kits. The system can track the delivery and create customs documents and receipts for the CKD kits from the assembling plant. The warehouse management system in mySAP Automotive can administer the kits as a whole as well as by component. This enables serial numbers to be tracked and allows for robbing to maintain production in the event of faulty parts. It sets optimal assembly sequences for the kits available. During assembly, the reporting points enable you to monitor progress and WIP (work-in-progress).

3.2.2 Solution Map for Automotive Suppliers

The Solution Map for automotive suppliers (*see* Table 3.2) illustrates the business processes supported by the mySAP Automotive Industry Solution.

For cross-industry areas of manufacturers and suppliers, mySAP Automotive offers a solution based upon the overall SAP strategy. Some functions correspond to the enhancements for manufacturers described above.

mySAP.com has been enhanced in the following areas for the supplier sector:

- Packaging logistics
- Processing of delivery schedules and subsequent functions

- EDI communication
- Optimization and tracking of transport
- Supplier Workplace
- Synchronization of production and delivery schedules

Packaging logistics

Packaging logistics enables packing regulations and multilevel packaging BOMs to be managed. It supports all the packaging processes in production and delivery. It enables goods receipt, goods issue and goods movements with packed materials. Packaging material is managed in special accounts, so that all partners always have an accurate overview of the packaging material available. Standard EDI messages enable you to compare and reconcile accounts.

Delivery schedules

The automotive system can process all forms of delivery schedules: normal, JIT, quantity and sequenced. It also handles special forms that are used internationally.

Sequenced production and delivery schedules

The schedule forms that have been used in the automotive industry for years are always based upon outline agreements on the delivery quantities of materials. The units actually scheduled result from standard material requirements calculations. The implementation of sequenced production and delivery schedules enables high-quality and high-cost systems to be ordered from the supplier with a direct reference to the end product. You can arrange just-in-time delivery of an ergonomic seat for a sports car or an exotic wood 'cockpit' for a luxury car directly to the assembly line.

EDI and ENX

Interfaces and preconfigured messages in mySAP.com can implement the standardized forms of communication defined by organizations such as VDA or ODETTE in the automotive industry.

Internet Marketplace

The automotive industry is currently reorienting itself. It is evaluating new forms of communication over the Internet to exchange information using standards such as ANX in the US or ENX in Europe, even though these standards are still being defined. mySAP.com also offers an automotive Marketplace for manufacturers and suppliers. The virtual Marketplace will not only handle information exchange, but also process inquiries, quotations, deliveries and invoices quickly and securely, without errors or paper, and in real time.

Transport and tracking

Planning, controlling and executing the delivery procedures used in the industry, such as just-in-time and sequenced, requires a large amount of time and effort. This is why special enhancements to the standard logistics functions have been developed. mySAP Automotive 2.0 can define routes, optimize trucks and loading and track transport via EDI or the Internet. These features simplify the typical, repetitive routes with the same type of goods that typify make-to-stock production in the industry. The solution aims at automating standard processes with as little planning and operating effort as possible. The system only presents exceptional situations to the user for processing.

Supplier Workplace

The Supplier Workplace (*see* Fig. 3.7) offers suppliers improved support for information procurement, particularly those companies who do not have their own comprehensive information systems. Suppliers can use standard Internet browsers to

TABLE 3.2   Automotive Suppliers Solution Map

Enterprise Management	Strategic Enterprise Management	Business Intelligence	Managerial Accounting	Financial Accounting		
Customer Relationship Management	Customer Service	Market Research & Analysis	Product/Brand Marketing	Sales Management	Sales Cycle Management	Sales Channels
Engineering Supplier	Engineering Projects	Product Engineering	Process Engineering	Target Costing	Product Data Management	
Supply Chain Planning & Monitoring OEM	Variant Demand Management	Resource Planning	Supplier Workplace	Supply Chain Monitoring		
Procurement Supplier	Strategic Purchasing	Operative Procurement	Inbound Logistics	Inventory Management	Billing	Vendor Performance
Manufacturing Supplier	Supply to Line	Manufacturing Execution	Quality Management	Manufacturing Confirmation & Monitoring		
Sales Supplier	Sales Planning	Sales Execution	Billing	Complaint Handling		
Spare Parts Business Supplier	Demand Management	Sales & Delivery	Backorders	Supply Network	Warranty	
Business Support	Human Resource Core Functions & Strategy	Human Resource Analytics & Enabling Solutions	Procurement	Treasury/Corporate Finance Management	Fixed Asset Management	

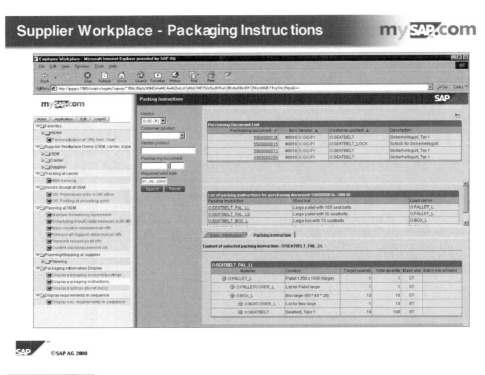

FIGURE 3.7   Supplier Workplace (© SAP AG)

track their release orders, deliveries and settlements in the manufacturer's system. The procurement and exchange of information becomes simpler and more cost-effective.

3.2.3 Solution Map for Sales and Service

Additional functions for sales and service are being developed. By the end of 2000, several projects will make the following functions available to respond to customer requirements:

- Vehicle dealers
- Import and distribution
- Spare parts
- Leasing and financing
- Guarantee and maintenance
- Repair-shop processing

In the future, the automotive solution will provide functions that enable the sale of individually configurable vehicle models over the Internet. It will enhance mySAP.com components such as mySAP CRM (Customer Relationship Management), mySAP BI (Business Intelligence) and mySAP SCM (Supply Chain Management) with industry-specific functions. This approach will link all forms of automotive sales to the production system.

The future release will customize existing functions or supply missing functions for spare parts, repair-shop processing, financing and leasing. New Workplaces will correspond to business roles and combine the functions of the mySAP.com solutions.

Vehicle Management System

The Vehicle Management System (*see* Fig. 3.8) serves as a good example of the additional development taking place for vehicle sales. The application enables importers and dealer organizations to manage all vehicles and carry out the necessary business functions. The Vehicle Management System manages a vehicle throughout its entire life cycle, from planning through order, production, delivery, sale and service. Enhancements to the standard system implement searching for vehicles in the production and delivery pipeline and define free configuration and the resulting pricing, status management, availability, delivery times and scheduling. These integrated functions enable the generation of a production order from sales information and a shipping notification from production information. The solution stores information about sold vehicles and makes it available for later service and support. Integration with

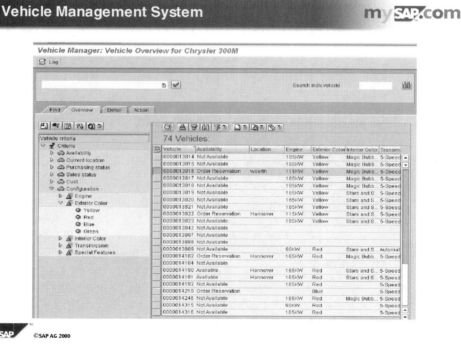

FIGURE 3.8   Vehicle Management System (© SAP AG)

mySAP CRM (Customer Relationship Management) builds the basis for market analysis, sales planning and customer retention.

3.2.4 Further Development

Further strategic development of mySAP Automotive will move in two directions. First, it will round off and complete the functions described above for processing variants in high-volume, make-to-stock production in the areas of engineering, supply chain management, purchasing, procurement and production.

Second, it will focus development activities on the new opportunities for business processes made available by the Internet. It will enhance existing functions, such as the Supplier Workplace and the Vehicle Management System, for vehicle sales. It will complete the range of services offered in the area of partner integration for development and supplier processes under the headings of collaborative engineering and collaborative planning. SAP regards the creation of industry-specific marketplaces as one of its primary business goals, and will continue to do so for the automotive industry. All players in the automotive market will find the Marketplaces an ideal forum to gather information about cars, trade vehicles and spare parts, or place advertisements in order to develop new business relationships or process existing business.

SAP will also focus on the development of the mySAP Automotive solution for sales and service. In close collaboration with strategic project partners from the automotive industry, this development will produce powerful solutions for automobile dealers, processing service and repair requests, and integrating the comprehensive solution for customer relationship management.

3.3 TWO SAMPLE APPLICATIONS

3.3.1 Automobile Manufacturers

Today, several automobile manufacturers use mySAP Automotive and its enhancements to support business processes in engineering, supply chain management, production, purchasing and procurement. To complete the overall solution, they also use the application components mySAP Human Resources and mySAP Financials.

The enormous improvements in processing large volumes of orders offered by mySAP Automotive 2.0, and its ability to work with APO 3.0, make the automotive solution even more suitable for automobile manufacturers with large throughput. Some of SAP's largest automotive customers put the solution into production in 2000.

To show the performance of mySAP Automotive, the following section lists the results of a performance test undertaken in mid-1999 at a large German automobile manufacturer.

Working with its customer, SAP developed and implemented a design for efficient requirements planning with the rapid planning matrix. The solution enables execution of planning runs (even subordinate planning runs) for highly variable products. It greatly enhances flexibility in production. The performance test completed all the requirements planning for 43,000 vehicle orders in less than 48 minutes. The test results exceeded the requirements of the customer.

The performance test was also the acid test for IBU Automotive's development model. This model plans for all strategic developments to be carried out in cooperation with a strategic development partner from the automotive industry. This ensures that the solution is suited for its purpose and stable.

3.3.2 Automobile Suppliers

The implementation of functions to process sequenced delivery schedules is a good example of enhanced SAP functions that are specific to the automotive industry.

For example: A manufacturer produces a vehicle model with the following variants: basic model, luxury version and sports version. The supplier produces seats for each configuration as normal, leather and sports seats. The sequence of bodies on the assembly line must be decided at short notice, because customers can change the configuration of their vehicles up to a week before delivery. The supplier receives information about which seat to supply only four to six hours before the assembly line requires the seat. The supplier has only a short time to assemble and deliver the seat.

Mapping this process in mySAP.com involves several steps.

1 Commercial outline data and planning
The manufacturer and the supplier agree on a long-term (usually one-year) purchase quantity, price and conditions. The SAP Sales and Distribution application component stores the basic information as an outline agreement. On a regular basis, monthly or weekly, the manufacturer informs the supplier of the planned numbers for vehicle production as a forecast delivery schedule. The supplier can use this information to plan and control materials procurement and pre-assembly. If required, the supplier can expand the information for use in JIT scheduling.

2 Control of final assembly and delivery
The actual control of final assembly for the seats is part of the sequenced forecast delivery schedule. This is a completely new development specifically aimed at the automotive industry. When the body reaches a specific point on the assembly line, the system triggers a shipping notification. At this point, the final configuration of the seat is known. Electronic data transfer transmits the delivery information to the supplier. The transmission includes the current delivery information, sequence of the required seats and additional control data. The supplier produces the seats

in the required form and loads them in the correct sequence. Delivery is made directly to the manufacturer's assembly line.

3 Settlement

Settlement occurs in a collective process (a daily collective delivery note). One invoice combines all the deliveries for a specific day. The conditions in the outline agreement and the quantity actually delivered provide the basis for the invoice. Individual settlement is impractical because the volumes involved are usually so high.

4 Control and evaluation

Because the processing involved here usually involves a huge amount of data that must remain available for later evaluations or reports, the executing system cannot store all the details itself. To free up the operating and administrative system, data is stored in SAP Business Information Warehouse (SAP BW). SAP BW stores and formats the data to determine identifiers for delivery performance, frequency of change or quality characteristics. Product costing and results analysis data also goes into this pool. In this case, the combination of standard functions, industry-specific enhancements and mySAP components offers an ideal solution to a very complex procedure.

References

Garel Rhys, *Automotive Industry Trends*. Presentation to the 15th Annual London Motor Conference, London, 14 May 1999.

Hermann Selzle, *Automobil Produktion 4/99*, Verlag moderne industrie.

Hermann Selzle, *Automobil Produktion 6/99*, Verlag moderne industrie.

mySAP Chemicals Industry Solution

Dr Walter Bäckert, Dr Rainer Frei and Gregor Wittreck, IMG AG, Business Unit Chemicals/Pharmaceuticals

4.1 A CHANGING INDUSTRY

Markets

To a higher degree than any other industry, the growth rate of the chemical industry depends upon overall economic performance. Increasing globalization makes not only domestic, but also international, markets increasingly important. For example, in the first half of 1999, two-thirds of revenue in the German chemical industry came from exports. The industry expected growth of 3.5 per cent in 2000. The high correlation between growth in the chemical industry and the gross domestic product of target countries derives from the wide range of use and multi-faceted nature of chemical products. In addition to basic chemicals, pharmaceutical products and chemical fibres, chemical products include insecticides, plant food, printing inks, paints, soaps, detergents and personal hygiene products.

The chemical industry in the US, Europe and Japan has an especially important economic role. In 1998, these regions alone earned about 73 per cent of worldwide chemical revenues, or approximately 1,244 billion euros (*see* Fig. 4.1). The earnings of the European chemical industry in 1998, approximately 433 billion euros, placed it third on the list of highest-earning industries, behind the food and automotive industries.

Although most people consider the pharmaceutical industry to be part of the chemical industry, this chapter does not deal with pharmaceuticals. The following discussion

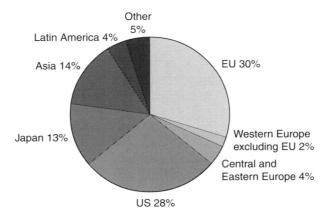

FIGURE 4.1   Worldwide distribution of chemicals production (© SAP AG)

concentrates on companies that exclusively produce chemicals, including basic and specialized chemistry.

4.1.1 Market Developments

Price is the only factor that affects competition in the basic chemistry industry. However, specialized chemistry allows a partial differentiation by specific product, knowledge of procedures and product quality. Despite positive economic forecasts, relatively slow growth and high cost and price pressures characterize the entire industry. Competitive pressure means that companies cannot always pass on increased prices for raw materials directly to their customers, or at least not the full amount.

To enable profitable business within this framework and to respond to the expectations of financial markets, three trends have appeared in the chemical industry. Each will become more pronounced in future.

▧ Concentration on speciality chemicals that allow for higher profits despite the high research and development costs and ever-decreasing product life cycles.

▧ Restructuring and rationalization of existing business areas to enable more rapid development, logistics and cash cycles and a reduction in overheads. This area includes networking with partners along the entire supply chain.

▧ Concentration on core business and the use of economies-of-scale effects to strengthen the tendency toward mergers, takeovers and globalization.

The use of individually tailored system solutions plays a central role in achieving the aims associated with these trends, particularly in implementing restructuring, rationalization, and economies-of-scale effects. Against this background, systems are not viewed purely as software, but along with strategies and processes, are regarded as an integrated unit to help a company reach its goals.

4.1.2 A Business Model in the Information Age

Recently, chemical companies have worked on optimizing their internal company processes. In the future, however, a company's ability to master cross-company processes will determine its success. In this context, complete supply chains, rather than individual companies, will compete with each other. The ability to become part of a network of suppliers and customers (networkability) increasingly becomes a critical factor in the success of a company. Companies must create the context for success at strategic and process level as well as at system level (Fig. 4.2).

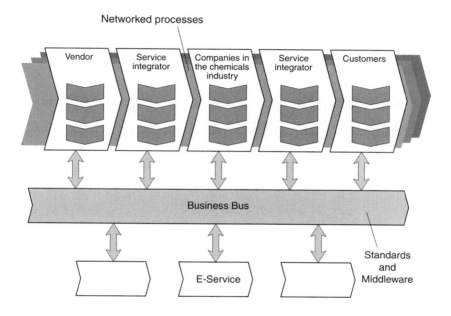

| FIGURE 4.2 | Constituent characteristics of the business networking model (© SAP AG) |

Characteristics of business networking

To meet the challenges of the future, the ability to cooperate, coordinate and communicate in innovation, supply chain management and customer relationship management is absolutely essential. Although designs for networking companies have been developed at the strategy and process level for years, the system support for this type of networking has only recently become available. For example, the Internet functions as a business bus by providing standards for the transfer and presentation of data. It also acts as the middleware that integrates cross-company processes with the necessary system and technical applications. The interplay of processes and applications results in seven trends that significantly influence the move to the information age (*see* Fig. 4.3).

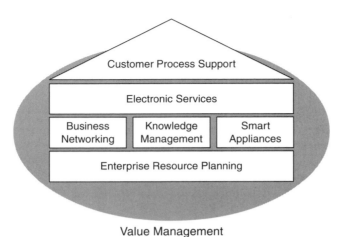

Value Management

FIGURE 4.3   Seven trends on the road to becoming a company ready for the Information Age (© SAP AG)

As in the past, enterprise resource planning (ERP) systems play a central role in planning and controlling business processes. Particularly as integrated systems, they can free companies from the burden of repetitive and administrative tasks. As a result, the market for ERP systems will grow by between 10 per cent and 20 per cent in the next five years.

Knowledge management systems can supply the information about customers, competitors, products and even processes themselves that companies require for seamless procedures.

Smart appliances will significantly influence business and private processes. Although no one can yet accurately estimate the multi-faceted character of smart appliances, satellite navigation systems, systems that measure point-of-sales information and sensor-based systems that measure wear and tear indicate the direction of future developments.

Business networking will remove the interfaces between companies. Network partners will automatically receive any important information they need. This information will be tailored to their specific requirements. Transfers between companies within the supply chain will flow easily, and the level of integration achieved will determine the success of the companies involved.

Electronic services make it possible to offload sub-processes to external partners or increase the effectiveness of a company by allowing it to use new services. The business bus allows a company to directly control and schedule external services. Examples of electronic services include product catalogues, goods exchanges and virtual marketplaces, such as the mySAP Marketplace.

New technologies enable a new dimension of customer process support. Companies have long sought to meet customer requirements when they design their products.

Companies in the Information Age can orient themselves directly to the needs of their customers. New technologies provide all the products, services and information that customers need to perform their tasks. Examples include helpdesk services and the use of customer relationship management systems.

Although using new technologies and services achieves a high level of rationalization, their use in systems is closely linked to a company's strategies and goals. In addition to financial goals, an orientation toward value as a central goal becomes increasingly important. Process measurement and data warehousing make it possible to measure non-financial concerns and therefore offer continual support for and control in reaching goals. Particularly for chemical companies, the creation of value both within a company and for its customers will become a success factor as companies move into the Information Age.

4.2 THE SOLUTION FOR THE CHEMICALS INDUSTRY

SAP products, particularly SAP R/3, are widely used in the chemical industry. More than 1,500 installations in 50 countries have made SAP the worldwide market leader for ERP systems in this industry.

Many installations originally included only the traditionally 'strong' R/3 application components such as Financials and Inventory Management. In Release 3.0, SAP took the first step toward comprehensive support of processes in the chemical industry. For example, the SAP Production Planning/Process Industry (SAP PP-PI) module developed into a powerful tool from being the 'smaller brother' of the SAP PP application component.

The increasing number of R/3 installations shows the success of the close collaboration between SAP, the chemical industry, its associations and consultants in the further development of SAP R/3. The Solution Map clearly illustrates SAP's claim to offer a strategic solution for the chemical industry.

4.2.1 Solution Map for the Chemical Industry

The requirements of the Information Age demand effective IT support that provides not only the implementation of software (packages), but also a comprehensive and integrated solution.

SAP R/3, enhanced with SAP products such as SAP Business Information Warehouse (SAP BW) and SAP Advanced Planner and Optimizer (SAP APO), forms the backbone of such a solution. Where SAP does not yet offer a solution, partner firms offer products that work with SAP R/3 over standard interfaces.

If, in SAP Production Planning, we examine short-term planning in addition to scheduling and optimization, the Solution Map offers three alternatives:

■ The capacity planning table in R/3, which offers no optimization function

TABLE 4.1 Chemicals Solution Map

Enterprise Management	Strategic Enterprise Management	Business Intelligence	Managerial Accounting	Financial Accounting		
Customer Relationship Management	Product Branding & Marketing	Prospecting	Selling	Servicing	Retaining	
Research & Development	Product Development	R&D Administration	New Technologies			
Plant Engineering	Facilities Management	Maintenance Planning	Maintenance Execution	Regulatory Compliance		
Process Engineering	Pilot & Technology Transfer	Quality Management	Regulatory Compliance	Operations Analysis		
Operations	Production Planning	Production Execution	Quality Management	Process Control		
Distribution	Logistics Planning	Transportation Execution	Regulatory Compliance	Tank & Warehouse Management	Procurement	
Business Support	Human Resource Core Functions & Strategy	Human Resource Analytics & Enabling Solutions	Procurement	Treasury/Corporate Finance Management	Fixed Asset Management	Environmental Health & Safety

- The production planning/detailed scheduling (PP-DS) module in SAP Advanced Planner and Optimizer

- Linking a partner product with the standardized Production Optimization Interface (POI)

Clearly, choosing one of these three alternatives does not depend solely upon the isolated requirements of short-term planning, but upon how a company wishes to plan its overall supply chain.

4.2.2 The Supply Chain in the Chemical Industry

Supply chains for chemical products are global. The Solution Map offers modules that cover processes and functions along the chain. Technical requirements often demand the distribution of functions throughout various regional or local systems. Nonetheless, the technology of application link enabling (ALE) provides integration into a global, virtual system. SAP R/3 offers standard functions for many scenarios, such as for master data management.

Vertical integration with the Plant Centric Solution

The following points list some of the factors that determine the quality of the supply chain:

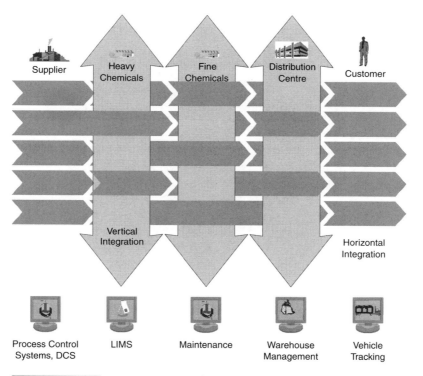

FIGURE 4.4   Horizontal and vertical integration (© SAP AG)

▦ The quality and availability of data that is relevant to planning, such as the data generated and summarized in distributed control systems and truck-tracking systems

▦ The timely transfer of changed planning data to the subordinate execution systems

SAP's 'Plant Centric Solution' addresses this vertical integration. In addition to R/3 application components (SAP PP, SAP MM, SAP WM and so on), it includes interfaces to special systems, such as distributed control system, work information systems and warehouse management computers (Fig. 4.4).

A sample process order procedure shows the aspects of process and data design that must be considered in order to achieve successful horizontal and vertical integration.

SAP PP-PI: Recipe, Process Order and Campaign

The process order forms the central data element of chemical (batch) processing. Fig. 4.5 illustrates the life cycle of a process order in the typical process steps of SAP R/3. The SAP PP-PI recipe is the master data and is copied as a template into the process order. (Recipe signifies a description of the structure of a product (the operations and components), with Process Instructions to communicate to operators.) A (multi-product) campaign can combine several process orders. This approach currently involves a manual step that Figure 4.5 does not reflect. Process orders can also map the required setup and cleaning steps.

Planning

The SAP PP-PI recipe includes all the information needed for requirements and capacity planning: it contains the material lists (ingredients, by-products and co-products) in addition to the procedural and production steps in use. If a tool such as SAP Advanced Planner and Optimizer (SAP APO) is used in sequenced planning, the recipes must be defined in an appropriate way to achieve integration and full functionality.

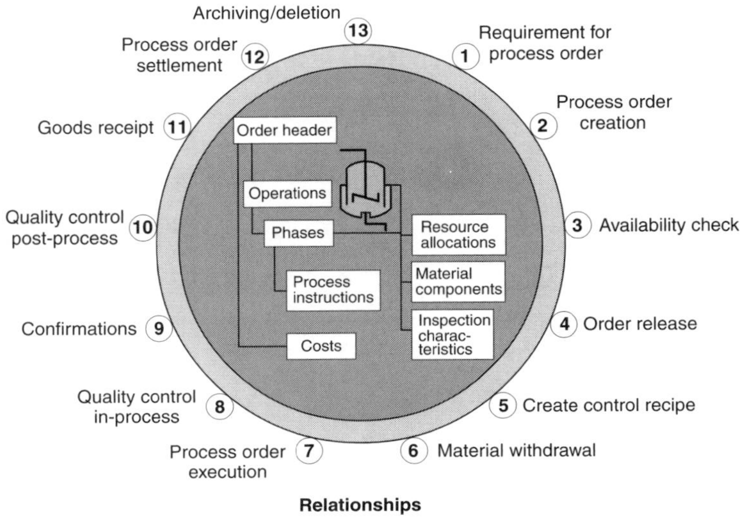

FIGURE 4.5   Sequence of a process order procedure (© SAP AG)

As a new feature, SAP APO Release 3.0 offers planning functions (similar to an optimizer for campaigns) and interfaces for SAP PP-PI master and transaction data. (SAP APO replaces the Process Flow Scheduler (PFS), which is no longer in development.)

Execution with process coordination

You can store detailed information about the phases of a recipe or process order, and then use it to generate a process specification or a control recipe. Release 4.0 of SAP R/3 greatly simplifies the maintenance of process specifications. The line operator handles the process specification interactively on the SAP R/3 monitor, entering the material used and the length of the procedure.

The system transfers the control recipe to the process control system. The control recipe contains information and default values (process order number and the quantity to be produced). It also indicates which data require confirmation. However, it is often impossible to store all the data required for process control in SAP R/3. Accordingly, even the high level of existing integration requires the maintenance of redundant recipes (in a manufacturing execution system, for example). In such a case, the R/3 recipe must be designed so that the process order can handle the aggregate operating data at the process control level (material movements, use of resources, and so on).

Calculation

SAP R/3 implements numerous special characteristics of chemical-specific calculation, such as cyclical and divergent material streams, production campaigns and so on (see References to this chapter). It uses the SAP PP-PI recipe for product costing. The process order permits a planned/actual comparison based upon acquisition postings, asset retirement postings and confirmations.

The requirements of the costing computer can differ from those of production if the costs for waste management, quality inspections, energy and handling have to be considered or if average rather than effective cleaning times are desired.

Additional areas

In addition to planning, execution, and calculation, the recipe and process order can store data for the following processes and functions:

- Criteria for batch determination
- Formulae to evaluate charge quantities (for deviations in yield from the pre-defined manufacturing step)
- Material provisioning
- Instruction for in-process quality inspections (IPC)

In addition to all these commercial and technical aspects, we must not forget the user – the user who enters or changes recipes during the daily maintenance of master data and adjusts process orders to the current situation. The design of the PP-PI recipe and the mapping of production processes in SAP R/3 must not underestimate the importance of the user. Communication between project teams and the ability to compromise are an absolute must.

4.2.3 Role-Based Design

SAP has not only made functional enhancements, but has also made the solution more user-friendly. As part of the EnjoySAP initiative, SAP has simplified and accelerated data entry and processing in many areas. Role-based design has the same effect because it combines typical functions. SAP R/3 contains pre-defined roles (*see* Fig. 4.6).

Sample: purchasing agent

With mySAP.com, the role-based mySAP Workplace functions as a portal. The Workplace gives purchasing agents access to:

- Standard SAP R/3 functions
- Vendor performance in SAP Business Information Warehouse (SAP BW)
- Planned requirements for key raw materials in SAP Advanced Planner and Optimizer (SAP APO)
- Quotations from cooperating partners (via SAP Business-to-Business Procurement)
- Marketplaces on the Internet to a wide range of suppliers of bulk goods
- Intranet and Internet for general information

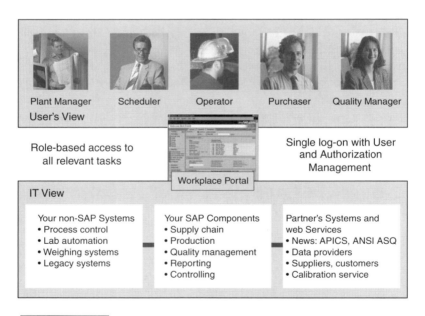

FIGURE 4.6   Role-based design (© SAP AG)

4.2.4 Further Development

The following developments are of particular interest to the chemical industry:

▨ The creation of a Marketplace in mySAP.com for MRO (material repair and over-haul) goods – a cooperative venture with SAP, the chemical and pharmaceutical industry and technical equipment suppliers

▨ Enhanced functions in the Environment, Health, and Safety module

▨ Creation of a recipe management system

▨ Mapping of recycling

▨ Posting divergent quantities during production (reconciliation)

▨ Bulk transport (from the mySAP Oil and Gas Industry Solution)

▨ Enhancement of SAP Advanced Planner and Optimizer (functions and integration)

▨ Redevelopment of the preconfigured chemicals solution and the ASAP implementation methodology

| 4.3 | **CASE STUDY OF SPECIALTY CHEMICALS** |

The Redipol Project at Ciba Specialty Chemicals – Polymers Division

The Performance Polymers Division of Ciba Specialty Chemicals in Basle, Switzerland, is a world leader in the development, manufacture and marketing of innovative polymers. Its core business consists of high-performance synthetics such as special materials based upon epoxy resins and other high-quality thermosetting plastics used by consumers and industry.

Increased prices and competition forced the Polymers Division to improve its cost structure and level of service at the beginning of the 1990s. To do this, the Redipol (re-engineering division, polymers) project came into being in 1992. Redipol's goals included the preparation of organizational structures and process flows for the European Economic Union. To reduce costs by one-third, the project had to re-engineer all business processes. The consequences were considerable:

▨ Thirteen regional logistics systems became one European logistics organization

▨ The 26 European warehouses were reduced to 6

▨ The product programme was restructured

▨ SAP R/3 was implemented throughout Europe

This is shown in Fig. 4.7.

The defining success factor for Redipol was the combination of business and systems knowledge in all phases of the project. The implementation of SAP R/3 took place in stages, beginning with the pilot installation in Scandinavia in 1993. SAP developed a modified R/3 Reference Model based upon the processes within Ciba Polymers. The second phase of the project in 1995–96 changed eight more European countries and four regional distribution centres (RDCs) over to SAP R/3. The project ended successfully in 1996 with solutions in place for direct delivery to customers (make-to-order), handling retail goods and controlling sales processes for deliveries outside the EU.

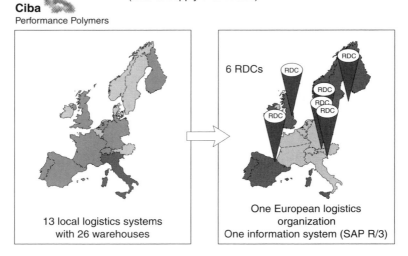

Annual cost reduction 22 million CHF
(22% of supply chain costs)

Ciba
Performance Polymers

6 RDCs

13 local logistics systems
with 26 warehouses

One European logistics
organization
One information system (SAP R/3)

FIGURE 4.7 Integration of the supply chain (© SAP AG)

Continuous
business
improvement

To take full advantage of the rationalization linked to the SAP R/3 implementation project, several smaller projects followed Redipol. Each had a clearly defined task and specific goals. Examples include improved accuracy of forecasts, optimization of tracking for campaigns and a reduction of floating capital for a specific product group. All project phases paid particular attention to measuring the results of the project. Participants could take important indicators directly from SAP R/3 with user-defined reports. The use of process cost accounting and a balanced scorecard system significantly enhanced the information-gathering process.

References

Verband der Chemischen Industrie e.V. (1997) *Chemiespezifische Kalkulation*, Schriftenreihe des Betriebswirtschaftlichen Ausschusses und des Finanzausschusses: 23.

mySAP Engineering & Construction Industry Solution

Bodo Wielsch, SAP AG

5.1 SPECIAL CHARACTERISTICS OF THE INDUSTRY

5.1.1 Engineering & Construction: an industry in itself?

Demanding challenges

Hardly any other economic sector contains such a varied range of companies as the engineering and construction sector. The complex development, construction and maintenance projects undertaken in this industry range from the construction of individual tool-making machines to the creation of complete industrial complexes. The projects must fulfil the requirements and criteria of customers under severe time and cost constraints. They also present the companies that carry out the projects with considerable technical challenges. To survive in the long term, engineering and construction companies must offer a wide range of products punctually and according to exact specifications. These companies need both technical expertise and organizational resources, especially because their customers expect a high degree of customization and innovation from them.

Customer orientation

The engineering and construction industry focuses on processes from specification to development, manufacture and acceptance. Today's global market offers great potential for orders in both the public and private sectors, as long as the companies know how to react flexibly to the needs of their customers. To do so, they must be able to react flexibly to changes during every phase of the product life cycle.

But does engineering and construction really exist as an independent industry? Or does the huge range of activities performed by companies in this area make it nothing more than a general store of individual companies? The following comments illustrate the connections between companies based upon an examination of construction. Many companies who are currently active in construction have grown organically into that area over the years. For the following reasons, consistent and detailed planning and implementation of the organizational development of these companies has only taken place in stages:

- Development of the current worldwide demand for construction could not have been foreseen in sufficient detail
- Companies had to use their strengths primarily to perform the tasks given in contracts; they did not expend it in sufficient quantities in their internal structure
- Little experience with planned company structures was available

Because of these factors, companies can still detect internal weaknesses that affect revenue and risk whenever they process construction orders.

The complexity of facilities and the demand for planned procedures strengthens the tendency toward distributed tasks. Primarily in the areas of customer decision-making and in the planning and project management that occurs after closing a contract, legally separate and independent speciality groups develop (consulting and engineering companies). These firms often develop along these two lines because of the split between engineering and construction in production companies.

Construction companies have also developed out of problems in the construction industry that arose because of the need for construction in the context of delivery facilities and because of the financial aspects of large orders. Even these cases do not exclude adjusting the company's organization to the requirements of order processing in engineering and construction.

Engineering companies

The largest group of installation companies developed from engineering companies. These companies first worked on the manufacture and operation of machines. Their customers, however, increasingly tended to work with closed production lines. This tendency forced production companies into delivering a choice of both partial and complete facilities.

Production companies in electrical engineering

Production companies in electrical engineering traditionally provide electrical components for machines and installations. Their specialization, unlike that of production companies in engineering, has not produced any market pressure to deliver partial or complete installations. In some cases, particularly when electrical components predominate, companies also deliver complete production installations.

Construction companies

Construction companies deal with building services for industrial facilities which are ready for immediate occupancy. If the construction portion of the facility predominates, construction companies also function as general contractors. If investment for the construction project, the type of facility and the construction requirements of a given country can provide sufficient revenue for a construction company, it may well accept orders outside the scope of its expertise to obtain a new and interesting contract. In this case, production companies in engineering and electrical engineering also function as suppliers.

Engineering companies

Engineering companies deal with the software involved in engineering and construction: design, planning, project management, the assignment of implementation tasks to machine and setup equipment suppliers, and supervision of the implementation.

For some orders, the type of services provided by engineering companies can differ between process-oriented and procedure-oriented engineering. Process-oriented engineering is based upon in-house knowledge for the design of the facility and the resulting processes. In procedure-oriented engineering, planning of the facility is based upon a design provided by a third party.

Experienced engineering companies can usually cover both partial aspects of a project and complete order processing, regardless of the complexity, scope, difficulty, location and technology involved.

Industry segments in SAP engineering and construction

If we consider the industry as a whole, mySAP Engineering and Construction includes the following segments:

- **Engineering and construction**

  Companies that manufacture industrial machines and equipment, including motors, turbines, oil drilling equipment, conveyors, power plants, ships and railroads

- **Engineering services and construction of large facilities**

  These firms work in project management and act as general contractors for the development and construction of highly complex facilities. This group primarily includes engineering, architecture and surveying

- **Principal and secondary building companies**

  These firms plan and construct complex construction projects such as buildings, building finishing, bridges and roads

5.1.2 Trends and Challenges

Profound structural changes

Over the last two decades, the engineering and construction industry has experienced profound structural change. The following factors characterize that change:

- Significant expansion of the scope of services
- Increased production of equipment for installations
- Increased ability of production units to provide services
- Increased complexity of projects and technology

Expanded scope of services

The expanded scope of services includes:

- Overall responsibility of construction companies for carrying out civil engineering projects

- Global assembly and startup

- Complete transportation and customs processing, from the manufacturing site to the construction site in the recipient country

- Training and customer personnel

- Startup of the installation

- Provision of production and quality guarantees

- Placement and procurement of experts to oversee the start of production and the operation of the installation

Complexity of projects

The most wide-ranging structural changes arise from relocating high-cost assembly work to plants in industrializing nations, massive increases in the value of orders for production units, and the complexity of the projects involved.

In most cases, this complexity arises not only from hardware deliveries (equipment parts, machines and units), but also from software deliveries (engineering, infrastructure, and so on). The complexity has reached a level at which the organizational challenges are greater than the technical challenges.

Agreements hide high risk

A single company cannot process such large projects alone. However, agreements between multinational companies involved in a project can lead to unforeseen problems and significant risks.

5.2 mySAP ENGINEERING & CONSTRUCTION INDUSTRY SOLUTION

Optimum tool

The establishment of a needs-based, flexible, and innovative system environment requires a tool that permits step-by-step refinement of a business strategy. SAP software:

Scope of SAP services

- Supports all phases of the product life cycle, from design to planning, assembly, acceptance, service and maintenance

- Permits strict monitoring of the customer service and maintenance phases that are critical to success

- Enables integration of the entire logistics chain

- Can be used across locations, companies and countries

- Supports a broad spectrum of organizational structures that make it possible to control supplier, subcontractors and customer logistics

The business environment in engineering and construction is fast-paced. It has never been so difficult to ensure the long-term success of a company. The efficient use of information provides the key to long-term competitive advantage. A high-performance information system paves the way to the goal of every activity in a company: profitability. Integrated business information systems create closely linked, global data networks, provide access to data networks, support business procedures and create a reliable basis for wide-ranging business decisions and this is what mySAP.com offers. In mySAP.com, SAP provides the data infrastructure that modern companies need to remain on course for success.

The specific business processes in individual industries are found in mySAP Industry Solutions, such as mySAP Engineering and Construction (SAP E&C).

mySAP E&C delivers the infrastructure and functions needed for worldwide integration and processing of logistics. SAP software supports cost control, contributes to increased revenue and tightens business flows. Companies get exactly what they need from an information system: solid and direct profitability.

The concept of lowering overall system costs has two aspects: the cost drivers from enterprise resource planning and a process that lowers costs to the lowest possible level while still permitting efficient and productive work. SAP supports companies in determining these costs throughout the entire life of an ERP system. This unified design avoids the trap of hidden costs.

5.2.1 Solution Map for Engineering & Construction

The Solution Map for Engineering & Construction shows how precisely and comprehensively mySAP.com maps the business processes of the industry. The Solution Map leads to accessible, integrated processes. Universal business processes replace traditional thinking along departmental lines and stress links to a company's management (Table 5.1).

Company management

mySAP Engineering & Construction offers a comprehensive range of functions for strategic planning, financial accounting, costing and cost accounting.

Customer service

A new understanding of the value of individual customers and the advantages of personalized customer service have contributed to the worldwide role of customer relationship management as the top topic among boards of directors. Suppliers who want to maintain their market position tomorrow must work today to build up efficient and effective relationships with their customers.

Product development

Product development in customer orders demands technical expertise and qualified employees. Research and development activities begin with ideas; a prototype or work description is the successful outcome of research and development activities. Design and testing constitute the central challenges, especially for the production of individual parts or tools.

Make-to-order

The customer stands at the centre of make-to-order production. The customer's needs and requirements become specifications for a tailored product. An order BOM lists the technical data processed and updated at each production step. In the end, the object of the BOM is the product at the time of its delivery to the customer.

TABLE 5.1 Engineering & Construction Solution Map

Enterprise Management	Strategic Enterprise Management	Business Intelligence	Managerial Accounting	Financial Accounting			
Customer Relationship Management	Market Research & Analysis	Marketing Program Management	Sales Management	Sales Cycle Management	Installation Management	Service Agreements	Service Fulfilment
	Project Management, Product Life Cycle Management (PLM), Quality Management						
Develop To Order	Design, Concept & Specification	Quotation & Contract Costing	Order Entry	Prototyping Product Development	Handover Contract Preparation		
	Project Management, Product Life Cycle Management (PLM), Quality Management						
Make To Order	Inquiry & Quotation Processing	Order Entry Processing	Manufacturing & Delivery	Warranty			
	Project Management, Change Management, Product Life Cycle Management (PLM)						
Engineer To Order	Concept & Product Development	Inquiry & Quotation Processing	Order Entry Processing	Procurement, Shipping & Assembly	Start Up & Warranty		
	Project Management, Plant Life Cycle Management						
Engineering Procurement Construction	Project Development	Engineering	Procurement	Construction	Commissioning & Start Up		
	Project Management & Configuration Management						
Construction	Marketing & Tender Acquisition	Bid Estimation & Contract Negotiation	Planning & Scheduling	Project Execution	Warranty & Post Construction		
	Contract Management, Configuration Management						
Service & Maintenance	Contract & Configuration Management	Acquisition & Sales	Maintenance Planning	Work Planning & Preparation	Order Processing	Setup & Warranty	
Business Support	Human Resource, Core Functions & Strategy	Human Resource Analytics & Enabling Solutions	Procurement	Treasury/Corporate Finance Management	Fixed Asset Management	Real Estate & Property Management	

This SAP Solution Map displays the range of business processes common to this industry.

Engineer-to-order

Products in engineer-to-order production are usually unique. Products are designed for a specific customer and have probably not been produced before. Construction, submission of quotations and cost estimates are the most important business processes here. BOMs and work plans for the entire product are created manually because of the uniqueness of the product. Engineer-to-order is usually extremely time-consuming. Project management tools can help to monitor and coordinate processing.

Industrial plant engineering and construction

Large plant and engineering construction projects create complete facilities which are ready for immediate occupancy based upon the requirements of customers. The principal business processes include cost estimates, creation of a conceptual design, optimization, planning, procurement, construction, picking, startup, maintenance and customer service. Industrial plant engineering and construction projects may have different planning and execution locations. These projects link cost accounting, revenue streams, profitability analysis, human resources and personnel planning to each other.

Building sector

The modern building sector must be able to react quickly to changes and competition. The *my*SAP E&C Industry Solution offers all the functions that construction companies need in order to secure their competitive advantage today; for example, logistics, human resources and project management.

Customer service and maintenance

Before a company can carry out installation or maintenance tasks, it must set the conditions for performing the service. For this reason, *my*SAP E&C creates work orders to produce costs, time, location and other contractual conditions. Documents and instructions stored in the system direct maintenance personnel to the required location and identify the technical data for the installations and devices that require maintenance or service. When the work is complete, the customer receives technical notes and a description of the work that has been carried out.

Supporting business processes

*my*SAP E&C offers high-performance functions for all the key elements of business support. Numerous features have been designed specifically for the special needs of the engineering and construction industry. These make it possible to manage and monitor human resources and payroll easily and efficiently. The features also make it possible to slim down procurement procedures and reduce inventories. There are also comprehensive functions for managing installations throughout their entire life cycle, including the simulation of changes of value and depreciation forecasts.

5.2.2 Two Scenarios in Detail

Make-To-Order Production

During make-to-order production, the requirements of the customer and the technical knowledge of the manufacturer combine to configure and cost a unique product. At this level, no complete specifications for the product can yet exist beyond the level of materials requirements planning. A cost estimate, however, can be derived from the BOM. Predefined guidelines help determine the probable costs and profit margin when the quotation is created. The profit margin serves as the criterion for deciding if the customer should receive a quotation at all. After receiving an order, the system compares the order to the quotation. It documents any changed resource needs for further use.

After approval of the changes, the order is released and the resources scheduled. Since the product structure has not yet been specified in its final form, order processing is likely to produce additional changes. The engineering change management component tracks any additional changes that affect cost, time planning or resource planning. Although individual assemblies are designed according to the requirements of specific customers, the manufacturer must be able to produce products that are then distributed across various orders. The system must transfer the characteristics of the configured parts to purchasing and production. In the interests of optimum production and procurement planning, companies can use the network as an MRP instrument in connection with the order BOM. The network also helps to coordinate the assembly of individual components or modules. Whether a company purchases individual parts externally or produces them internally depends upon the quantity required, the price and the delivery date. After it is produced, the product is delivered to the customer and installed on site. The product specifications form the basis for the delivery of spare parts and maintenance required. Here, companies should also apply regulations as and when necessary.

Industrial Plant Engineering and Construction

Suppliers in industrial plant engineering and construction processes place construction in the context of large domestic and international projects. The most important business processes include engineering, procurement and assembly. Plant construction companies design and construct civil engineering projects, facilities that involve technical procedures (including power plants and process manufacturing plants), transportation routes and systems and water treatment facilities. These types of projects usually require significant development and administrative efforts. The general contractor is responsible for all phases of a construction project and works together with several subcontractors and suppliers, including manufacturers of individual components, suppliers, construction companies and construction-related companies. The management of these project partners plays an important role in the project.

mySAP E&C provides immediate access to information about customers, interested parties and completed projects. The system guarantees quick and seamless access to all the data that a construction company needs. Companies can manage complex construction projects only with an integrated project system. mySAP.com can map all the procedures involved, from an initial inquiry to the end of the contract. mySAP E&C offers functions for cost projections, quotations, planning services, schedules, resources, costs and finances. The functional scope may also increase after the project starts. However, preliminary data can provide a good estimate of the cost framework.

The startup phase procures quotations for materials and services from various suppliers, especially in cases involving long lead times for material staging. Here, the SAP functions for electronic data interchange (EDI) and external procurement give a construction company a competitive advantage. Companies can even maintain several versions of a quotation. After the order is received, the operating budget, schedule and processing plan are created in the Controlling and Project System application components.

In this phase, the sales organization transfers the order to project management. Doing so triggers all the measures needed to process the project in the specified time and cost-frame, including engineering, procurement, delivery, manufacture and assembly. Planning construction projects requires the creation of numerous documents (plans, specifications, technical drawings and so on). A CAD system closely linked to mySAP.com can map the structure of the facility. An integrated document management system ensures that all documents are consistent and the most up-to-date version is always available.

Planning is also made easier by linking materials management (building supplies and services from subcontractors, for example) and assembly. As the project develops, it updates the data and project structure incrementally from the planning phase. mySAP E&C offers maximum flexibility by mapping vendors and customers as needed. It supports all invoice types that are commonly used in the industry. Since execution of a project can occur in several countries, accounting can handle multiple currencies.

At the beginning of a project, the structure of the facility has not yet reached its final form. Changes during construction are unavoidable. The engineering change management component comes into play to manage the changes and to log them for follow-up management. As in make-to-order production, changes have direct effects on costs, scheduling and resource planning. Simulation variants can store different versions of the structure. Given small profit margins and increased cost pressures, constant monitoring of the construction site represents an important task. During setup and management of the construction site, companies can use mySAP.com solutions to access intranets and the Internet. Entry of time data serves as a good example. Revenue streams can be displayed according to quantity-based cost accounting and individual sites.

Companies can use freely-defined criteria to combine data across construction sites and thereby create consolidated areas. In addition to project monitoring and control at the operating level, mySAP Engineering & Construction can also map the entire life cycle of a facility in the system. The information already available can be used in integrated form for subsequent business processes such as sales, maintenance, warranties and re-engineering. mySAP E&C offers a comprehensive, real-time overview of schedules, resources and tasks. Costs and finances are always transparent; companies can track and implement changes during the life of the project.

5.3   COLLABORATION – CROSSING BORDERS WITH mySAP.com

Cross-company cooperation throughout the entire life cycle

Until recently, the main task of product data management (PDM) consisted of creating links between technical and business information, between construction and production. The age of the Internet, however, brings new challenges. Various types of direct collaboration must replace the traditional division of internal and external users in the logistics chain. In addition, users want a needs-based work environment that is tailored to their individual requirements and which offers access to relevant systems, processes and information.

SAP Product Lifecycle Management is the solution. As an integrated component of mySAP.com, it offers PDM users Internet-supported access to product and process data during the entire product life cycle. Access occurs through the mySAP Workplace, an open portal with all the information and applications required for effective work in a dynamic, market-oriented environment. The Workplace also enables cross-company, integrated cooperation with business partners over an individual, adjustable, easy-to-use interface.

To enhance individual productivity, the mySAP Workplace (*see* Fig. 5.1) combines SAP applications and external applications with Internet software and services. All the functions can also be called up directly from the SAP system from Easy Access Menus.

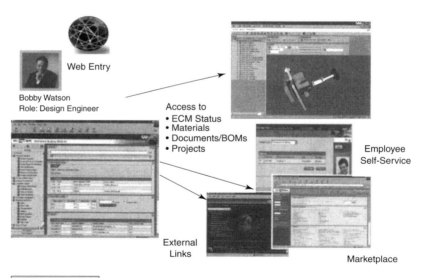

Web Entry

Bobby Watson
Role: Design Engineer

Access to
• ECM Status
• Materials
• Documents/BOMs
• Projects

Employee
Self-Service

External
Links

Marketplace

FIGURE 5.1   The mySAP Workplace (© SAP AG)

As an integrated ERP solution for product data management, mySAP Product Lifecycle Management supports the user throughout the entire production life cycle: development, sales, production and individually-tailored services.

Comprehensive use of the Internet also enables direct links between all the business

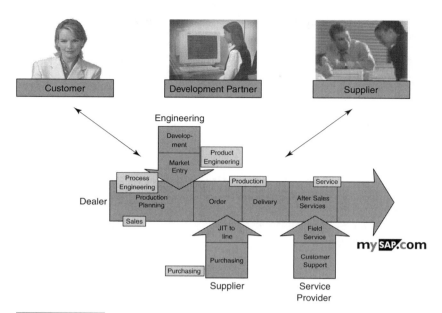

FIGURE 5.2   Cross-company cooperation and perfect visualization with the engineering workbence (© SAP AG)

partners in the extended supply chain, whether they are customers, vendors or development partners. mySAP Product Lifecycle Management offers an ideal platform for all PDM users inside and outside the company. The solution, however, is far more than just an integrated system for managing the product life cycle. It includes a standard, universal data model for product, process and resource data in all phases, from design through production to service (Fig. 5.2).

The product variant structure (PVS) used by companies in combination with traditional structures, BOMs and work plans, has particular importance. It enables companies to map a structure with the help of functional nodes and has a special display procedure for the structure of products with numerous variants. After expansion, the nodes create a multilevel hierarchy that displays a clear product structure, including materials.

mySAP Product Lifecycle Management provides a unique basis for cross-company, integrated cooperation between all partners in construction, both internally and externally. The following examples indicate the breadth of the platform.

Shortening the lead time of products can only succeed with hard work by the employees responsible, who work with CAD design, BOMs and work planning, to simultaneously process new or changed products.

mySAP Product Lifecycle Management creates the foundation required for simultaneous processing with the Engineering Workbench, a new maintenance environment for product and process data. Users employ complex search criteria to record various BOM and work plan objects into their work lists, without 'locking' the objects. An object is locked only when a component or procedure must be changed. Other users

Collaborative engineering with mySAP.com

Simultaneous construction and perfect visualization with the engineering workbench

can still work with the remaining structures, such as BOMs, simultaneously. The integrated Viewer in the Engineering Workbench makes it possible to display 3D models, and to enlarge or reduce parts of the models. Should this feature prove insufficient, SAP R/3 can manage individual parts of a product structure along with their installation locations, and permits visualization with digital mock-up (DMU).

For example, you can assemble a part step-by-step by simply selecting the required component for each validity date. Integrated functions for redlining, electronic marking and comments are available for drawings.

Integrated change and life-cycle control

Complex change processes often involve or affect several users and departments. mySAP Product Lifecycle Management supports the submission, checking and release of changes, change requests and change orders. All the important PDM objects are linked to these functions for change control.

Consistency in all worksteps

SAP Business Workflow enables the fast and seamless exchange of work packages between the employees responsible and provides a collection of samples in this area.

Scaled release of costing, planning and production changes occurs much like the change status of current release orders. Proposed changes undergo simulation and comparison with individual company regulations before the system generates an order. These check rules can issue a warning before deletion of a procedure, or issue an error warning when confirming a procedure.

SAP R/3 supports all the central logistics processes, from the design of a product to sales and any subsequent maintenance. These processes correspond to the various phases of the product life cycle. In the process, the product structure begins as a design and sales structure, changes into a plan or construction structure, and finally becomes a maintenance structure.

A large number of departments and users participate in a product's life cycle, working with product data, product management, development, work planning, requirements planning, purchasing, sales and service. Configuration management manages the product in all its phases. All the users involved can access the same data. Configuration management uses a meta-object, a product file, to manage a product. This can be created at any time, and then assigned to a life cycle already defined in Customizing.

A product file can create as many versions of a life cycle phase as required. When you create a new version, you can select the previous version; when the product enters a new phase, you can once again define the previous version. This process results in a network that depicts the creation and development of the product.

Fast, informal inter-company cooperation

Development and construction projects must guarantee direct and informal communication between all participants, regardless of their status as employees, customers, vendors or development partners. All require access to the relevant project data, product data and documentation. The opportunity to change or add comments to project plans and documents must also exist. Traditional communications, such as fax or e-mail, are relatively slow; as the number of participants in the project grows, the chances of confusion and errors increase. Security considerations move many companies to limit their partners' access to internal PDM systems (Fig. 5.3).

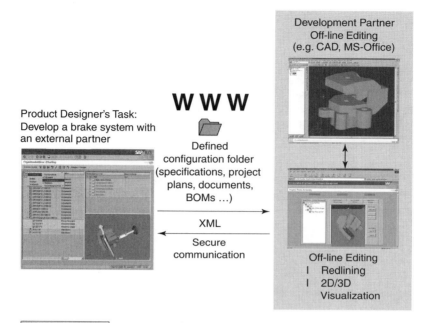

Product Designer's Task:
Develop a brake system with
an external partner

W W W

Defined
configuration folder
(specifications, project
plans, documents,
BOMs ...)

XML

Secure
communication

Development Partner
Off-line Editing
(e.g. CAD, MS-Office)

Off-line Editing
I   Redlining
I   2D/3D
    Visualization

FIGURE 5.3   Construction and project management across companies (© SAP AG)

The Collaborative Engineering application offers an Internet-supported platform for development and construction projects. An Internet browser provides all partners with access to relevant project information. They can display, change and comment on objects in the SAP R/3 without changing the objects themselves. Existing documents can be changed or new ones added. Once the server confirms the change status, all partners see it immediately. The operating data in SAP R/3 are not changed. The project manager can use configuration management to export specific product or project structure data from the SAP system, and thereby ensure data consistency.

A plug-in is provided to visualize process data over the web server. Whenever changes occur in Collaborative Engineering, an import and comparison mechanism loads the new structure into SAP R/3.

Links with the ERP functions in mySAP.com enable mySAP Product Lifecycle Management to integrate all processes in product data management into a higher-level system for development, planning, production, distribution and accounting. The modular character of mySAP.com also allows the use of PDM in distributed, technically independent systems. In this case, communication occurs over SAP Application Link Enabling (ALE). The use of ALE can distribute material masters, BOMs and documents (including the originals) over loosely linked systems.

Inside a system:
SAP PLM offers
versatility

References

VDI-Gesellschaft Entwicklung Konstruktion Vertrieb (Ed.) (1991) *Auftragsabwicklung im Maschinen- und Anlagenbau*, Schäffer Verlag für Wirtschaft und Steuern.

mySAP Insurance Industry Solution

Hans-Dieter Scheuermann and Jürgen Weiss, SAP AG

6.1	**A CHANGING INDUSTRY**

Markets

Market economies can be very unpredictable. Many European insurance companies have learned this lesson in the recent past. After decades of regulation and the partitioning of national markets by state supervisory agencies, the insurance industry saw the publication of the White Book by the European Commission on the Single Insurance Market in the mid 1990s. Liberalization aimed at opening up the market and eliminating governmental regulations that had previously hindered commerce in financial services. As a result, many insurers are now faced with worldwide competition.

Germany, where the premium income of primary insurers makes it the second largest European insurance market, provides a typical example of the changed context. Prior to 1994, the regulatory agency responsible for the supervision of the insurance industry ensured a relatively homogeneous product and price structure. Authorities claimed the right of preventative rate approval, which particularly handicapped the life, health and car insurance sectors. Since deregulation, state supervisory agencies have moved towards creating and subsequently implementing controls on abuse.

Similar trends toward deregulation have developed outside Europe. For example, in the US, the White House and Congress have agreed on a new law that repeals the Glass-Steagall Act of 1933. That law arose as a direct result of the stock market crash of 1929. To protect customers and investors, the law mandated *de facto* separation of banks, investment firms and insurance companies. In Japan, where the premium income of primary insurers makes it the second largest insurance market in the world (after the US), regulation has been unable to avoid liberalizing the inefficient domestic insurance market. Protection of the domestic economy from foreign competition has had the result of making Japanese companies lag behind global development.

Strategies

Less regulation also means more freedom for setting prices and offering products: that is, more competition. Insurers have reacted to these developments with various strategies. Their strategies primarily depend upon local market conditions and their own market position. Some insurers have attempted to equalize the market by a differentiated price and product policy. In many European countries, customers have difficulty gaining an overview in the sector for car insurance because of pricing structures that cannot easily be compared. Other companies attempt to find their salvation by concentrating on their core competencies and thus be regarded as niche suppliers. Insurers involved with special products outside mainstream business appear to have found success with this strategy.

Deregulation has also resulted in increasingly aggressive competition where price is concerned. Many insurers have recently seen themselves forced to lower prices or develop a direct insurance offer because of intensive competition and the appearance of new competitors such as direct insurers. Two factors often make price wars the only option for companies. They cannot grow from their own resources and decades of partitioning have left them with large capital cushions. Yet price wars can lead many incorrectly positioned or weakly capitalized companies to a dead end.

According to the observations of the German Insurance Association (Gesamtverband der Deutschen Versicherungswirtschaft) price and tariff competition increasingly affects commercial and private risks (Fig. 6.1). Many experts fear that some companies in this increasingly difficult market environment might put the income they earn from

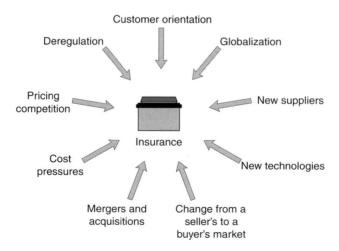

FIGURE 6.1   Trends in the insurance market (© SAP AG)

spinning off reserves into competition. Various business and capital policies result in reserve quotas that vary considerably. When the reserve capital no longer covers losses, these companies will disappear.

In the meantime, many insurance companies have modelled themselves on industrial companies and are trying to control their costs. In a study of the European insurance market by Datamonitor, the British market research institute, most companies interviewed admitted that cost reduction was the primary part of their business policy. Topics such as lean management (flat hierarchies), lean production (modular systems in the range of insurance offered), controlling and company-wide risk management or outsourcing have long since been popular with the boards of directors of insurance companies.

Customer relationship management (CRM) represents the second most significant aspect of policy. Since product differentiation in the fast-paced financial sector becomes increasingly difficult, companies rely more and more on service and orientation to customers. Almost 48 per cent of customers who purchase insurance for commercial vehicles have changed insurers at least once. Reasons for doing so include high prices and unsatisfactory service when a loss occurs. It is no wonder, then, that assistance services, such as products for tourists who encounter problems when on vacation, are now part of the service repertoire. In the UK, the commercial vehicle sector has long included loss management as part of its active service standard. After an accident, customers can use it to make an appointment at a garage or to hire a car. As a side effect, companies also save money with this form of management since they negotiate agreements with the other firms involved.

Mergers and acquisitions offer another way to reduce costs. It is primarily the global players in the insurance industry who choose this option to produce economies of scale. Guaranteed premiums become a guarantee of survival in the market. Companies which follow this policy include the German firm, Allianz, and the French firms AGF, GAN and Groupama. Also consider the merger of four German companies into Ergo, now the second largest insurance group in Germany. The list of recently merged companies is a long one.

Industry observers expect to see increased thinning out of the market in the future, even beyond national borders. Given the diversified market structure in Europe, the probability of such a development is very high. Even AXA-UAP, the largest European life and retirement insurer, has only a 6.5 per cent share of the European insurance market. Mergers and acquisitions offer an alternative to the expensive and risky setup of sales networks in other countries.

This trend does not apply only to insurance companies, as the $72 billion merger of Citibank and the Travelers Group into the financial group known as Citygroup makes clear. The trend toward companies that offer all financial services is growing and hits insurance companies with more competitors: banks. Banks have cast an envious glance at insurance customers and can play their trump card: a high market presence. This trend toward banking insurance leads to financial institutions taking over insurance companies so that they can offer insurance products in their branches.

Occasionally, however, the pendulum swings in the other direction. The German industry leader Allianz uses its participation in the German Dresdner Bank and the Spanish Banco Popular to turn tellers' windows into another distribution channel. This type of distribution may well become even more significant in future. In Spain, about 70 per cent of new Allianz insurance policies are purchased at banks. Many insurers follow an aggressive strategy toward banks with their activities in asset management. The German leader has also reached the top here; it has defined asset management as an area of core competency, along with traditional insurance activities. Within its own company, the Allianz Group manages capital assets of about $335 billion, and has its eye on both institutional and private bank customers who are prepared to change.

New technologies   After an investment blockage caused by the year 2000 bug, the modernization of IT and communications networks will become the decisive competitive criterion for many insurers over the next few years. Without a highly-developed IT system, the flexibility and speed that companies need to reach competitors or meet customer wishes cannot exist. At the top of the wish list of IT managers in European insurance companies is efficient customer relationship management (CRM). This situation is the logical consequence of increasing market, competitive and cost pressures. Insurance companies seek to take products and services away from competitors, to optimize their marketing, distribution and service processes, to win new customers, retain existing customers and expand the range of services they offer. Customer life cycle management is a popular topic, but must be accompanied and optimized by suitable products.

In concrete terms, these developments mean that insurance companies must leave behind the process-oriented view which fails to consider customer needs and adopt a customer-oriented view which includes individually-tailored products, services and communications. Companies that can reinvent themselves in this manner will find a wealth of decisive competitive advantages. The change will also have technological consequences for information systems, which must offer the following:

- Immediate access to all relevant information
- Central access to information from various internal and external sources
- Standardized communications
- Coverage of all business processes
- A centralized view of customer and business partner data
- Personalization of products and services, along with a better understanding of customer needs
- Shorter development cycles for products and services (time-to-market)
- A centralized view of customers
- Flexibility and independence when selecting distribution channels by using new communications media
- Optimization of existing distribution and service contracts

The need for action by insurance companies is clear. Above all, they must establish and expand communication centres such as call centres and the Internet. They need data warehouse and CRM applications such as activity management or customer segmentation. They must link existing and new insurance solutions to the back office.

The explosive dynamism of the Internet almost seems to have passed by European insurance companies. In Germany, for example, the industry hosts about 140 websites that only offer information. There is no such thing as a policy available to download from the web; online purchases of insurance are still forbidden because, by law, customers must receive certain information on paper. Clearly, this restrictive situation must change in the medium term.

According to the Datamonitor study, two-thirds of insurance companies that do not yet offer Internet policies want to do so within the next two years. The low transaction costs and the attractive demographics of Internet users (65 per cent are between 25 and 49 years old) mean that the Internet could develop into one of the most significant distribution channels for the insurance industry. The effect of 'cannibalization' with other distribution channels, such as the traditional sales force, may occur, but will probably have effects far less serious than many suppose. Complicated products that require explanation are no better suited to distribution over the world wide web than providing support for large-scale customers.

American analysts such as Morgan Stanley and Dean Witter see not only opportunities for the insurance industry with web technology, but also risks. New competitors from outside the industry, such as Intuit or Yahoo!, have already entered the market in the US. Vertical portals – virtual insurance markets with a broad range of services – increase the transparency of prices and replace traditional intermediaries such as brokers or insurance agents, or at least increase the pressure on margins and premiums. After deregulation, the Internet might push the industry into even more competition.

Summary

Insurance companies can only exist in an increasingly complex market environment if they offer a broad and customer-specific portfolio of products and services and when they include as many distribution channels as possible. Flexibility, efficiency and performance are as decisive as expansion into new markets and openness to new alliances. All these success factors rest upon an IT infrastructure which has integrated business information available throughout the company. Mastery of modern technology will separate the winners from the losers.

6.2 THE SAP SOLUTION FOR INSURANCE

A look back

SAP also has experience among insurance companies. As early as the 1980s, SAP had more than 50 insurance customers, primarily German. Since the mid 1990s, SAP has significantly expanded its standard software towards the needs of the insurance industry. The already strong involvement of SAP in the insurance sector was strengthened further in 1997 with the founding of the Industry Business Unit (IBU) Insurance. Today, around 340 insurance companies in more than 25 countries use SAP solutions. SAP provides its current and future customers with new components for its mySAP Insurance Industry Solution (*See* Fig. 6.2). To respond effectively to the needs of the market, SAP cooperates closely with pilot customers from the insurance industry in early development phases.

SAP Business Framework

The SAP Business Framework provides the framework for the Insurance Solution. To SAP, the Business Framework represents a component-supported, integrated family of products. The architecture of the Business Framework rests upon object-oriented, open interfaces, Business Application Programming Interfaces (BAPIs), which enable distributed business process scenarios. A central Business Object Repository makes the relevant business objects, and the methods that work with them, available to customers and partners. The advantages of this architecture include multi-faceted integration possibilities within a heterogeneous system landscape, the ability to adjust flexibly to new technologies or applications, and protection for investment because of lower upgrade costs and open interfaces. The Business Framework also enables insurance customers to replace their traditional, sector-oriented approach with a modern, function-oriented, cross-product approach.

SAP business partners

In addition to the Business Framework, all mySAP Insurance components are based on a central business partner concept that enables a cross-process view of data. This feature allows insurance companies to store all partner data in a database, regardless of the

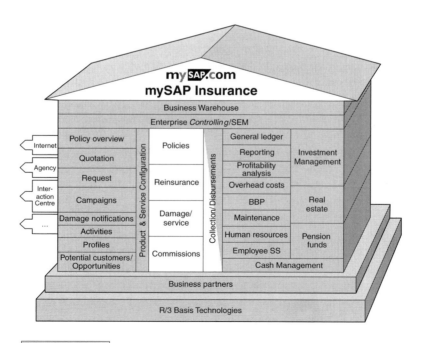

FIGURE 6.2   SAP Solutions in insurance companies (© SAP AG)

type of business relationship involved, without any data redundancy. Business partners can play various roles (for example, interested party or customer), or have relationships to other business partners. Companies can even map familiar relationships in this manner and use them in a business context. One typical scenario involves insurance contracts with several beneficiaries.

Back-office applications

Generally speaking, the individual components of the mySAP Insurance architecture can be assigned to both the front and back office areas. The development of the mySAP Industry Solution began in the business support environment, whose individual applications can be divided into management systems (such as Financials or Procurement) and investment systems (such as Cash Management or Property Management). SAP meets customer requirements for efficient capital asset management by providing a broad range of investment management systems.

To position themselves successfully with other financial service providers, insurance companies need effective solutions to monitor and control short-, medium- and long-term revenue streams. Close cooperation with the independent mySAP Banking Industry Solution secures valuable development synergies for SAP's insurance customers. SAP customers have been well served by integrated management systems such as Human Resources or Accounts Payable for many years.

Collections and disbursements

As an insurance-specific sub-ledger accounting system, IS-CD (Collections & Disbursements) acts as the interface between core insurance applications, such as commission management, and other more or less industry-specific business support systems. Here, too, the components reflect the Business Framework; SAP has implemented a basic separation of calculation and settlement systems. External systems known as operational systems determine the size of contributions and premium requests and their due dates or payments due to claims for damages. In contrast, IS-CD operates as a settlement system that manages postings, controls payment transactions and handles debt collection and late payment.

Claims management

The new insurance component for Claims Management (IS-CM) works within the Business Framework and consists of a front-office part for claims management and a back-office part for financial procedures. Functionally, the solution covers the entire claims management process, from incoming notification to the implementation of recovery clauses or revenues from regressions. The design philosophy includes various interfaces for different types of users (call centre employees, for example) and structured facts capture. The product also uses new business-to-business concepts such as links to external service providers.

Commissions

The new Commissions system (IS-CS) enables insurance companies to use monetary incentives to motivate their sales force and to manage the corresponding procedures and data. It includes all the familiar forms of commissions, such as brokerage, profit sharing, bonus loading, reserves and cancellations. The system works across sectors, so financial institutions can also use it. Insurance companies can create their own valuation, calculation and distribution rules. The solution also makes it possible to represent hierarchies and revisable commission accounting.

CRM

mySAP Customer Relationship Management (CRM) enables insurance companies to place their customers at the centre of their business processes. Regardless of the communications channel, or touchpoint, used, insurance companies can address customers individually and react to their specific needs. In addition to the existing SAP Business Partner and Business Information Warehouse components, IBU Insurance will offer a range of CRM solutions that provide insurance companies with various options for interaction and instruments for controlling marketing and distribution (Fig. 6.3). These instruments include a Customer Interaction Centre, a user interface for call centre employees, and functions for campaign, contact and activity management.

The Business Framework philosophy also plays an important role here. This is because, to maintain a centralized customer view, the operating applications must be linked to CRM functions via a technical connectivity layer, such as HTML (Hypertext Markup Language) or XML (eXtensible Markup Language). Many customer processes do not end at the CRM layer (displaying business partner data, for example), but access data directly (when enhancing a contract, for example). This IT encapsulation of applications provides insurance companies with a stable and efficient IT strategy.

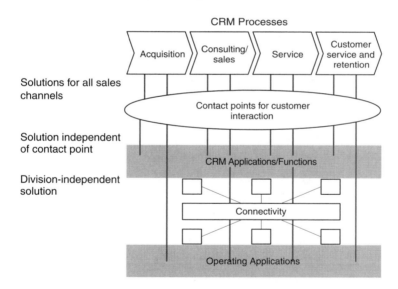

FIGURE 6.3   mySAP CRM (© SAP AG)

mySAP.com

The latest addition to the SAP product family is mySAP.com. This e-business platform combines various Internet-based applications such as e-commerce scenarios, a web portal (also with industry-specific features) and outsourcing options. With mySAP.com, SAP offers innovative insurance companies the ability to provide their customers, vendors, brokers or agents with new interaction channels that are available around the clock. The platform also includes Workplaces with role-based menus. For example,

TABLE 6.1 Insurance Solution Map

Enterprise Management	Strategic Enterprise Management	Business Intelligence	Managerial Accounting	Financial Accounting		
Customer Relationship Management	Customer & Prospect Management	Agency & Broker Management	Direct Business Management	Relationship Marketing Management	Sales Management	
Marketing & Product	Market Research & Analysis	Risk Analysis	Premium Calculation & Rate Setting	Product Development		
Sales	Commissions	Sales Support	New Business & Renewals	Business Development	Sales Controlling	
Operational Management	Policy Management	Commission Management	Claims Management	Reinsurance	Pension Funds Administration	Collections & Disbursement
Investment Management	Asset Allocation	Portfolio Management	Portfolio Accounting	Controlling & Performance		
Business Support	Human Resource Core Functions & Strategy	Human Resource Analytics & Enabling Solutions	Procurement	Treasury/Corporate Finance Management	Fixed Asset Management	

This SAP Solution Map displays the range of business processes common to this industry.

claims managers can use the Workplace as a web interface to access their most important business processes, internal information and external information.

Business
Intelligence

mySAP Business Intelligence components, such as SAP Business Information Warehouse (SAP BW) and SAP Strategic Enterprise Management (SAP SEM) form the top level of SAP architecture for insurance companies. SAP SEM supports value-oriented management with the following components: Business Consolidation (SEM-BCS), Business Planning and Simulation (SEM-BPS), Business Information Collection (SEM-BCS), Corporate Performance Monitor (SEM-CPM) and Stakeholder Relationship Management (SEM-SRM). SAP BW is an independent application environment that procures, summarizes and selects information from various sources and makes the results available as queries, evaluations and analyses.

Solution Map

The Solution Map, which is updated annually, provides a process-oriented overview of the entire mySAP Insurance solution. You can find the most current version on the insurance pages of the SAP website (www.sap.com). The Solution Map aims at finding a common language with insurance customers and at enabling partners and customers to participate in SAP development. SAP does not want to develop all the applications itself. The Solution Map indicates the areas for which licensed development partners already provide solutions. A second level of the Solution Map shows the sub-processes involved (Table 6.1).

6.3   SAMPLE APPLICATIONS

Incomplete
integration

Made-to-order, individual developments dominate the IT landscape of insurance customers who decide to implement SAP solutions. Due to the incomplete or unsatisfactory integration of varied sub-systems it usually requires several interfaces to move data from sub-ledger accounting into the general ledger. Companies therefore find it difficult to obtain an overview of their financial status and the liquidity of the company (*see* Fig. 6.4). Effective controlling is almost impossible without an integrated system.

Fewer interfaces

Companies can reorganize the value flow only when they consolidate their pre-loaded data systems (such as those for claims management) and separate those systems from settlement systems such as collections and disbursements. This approach lets companies position their operational systems for calculations and IS-CD as a settlement system and greatly simplifies the interface landscape (*see* Fig. 6.5). In addition, this approach lets a company supply internal and external accounting data via a central interface; it provides a single source of entry.

The reduced cost of exchanging information between various IT systems was the primary motivation behind the decision of a large Swiss insurance company to implement SAP. The company simultaneously reaped the benefits of the comprehensive and international reporting options of the new software, which gave it an integral view of all relevant company procedures. The background for the decision included the diverse

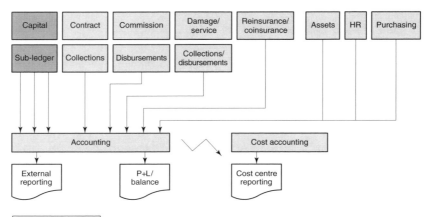

FIGURE 6.4   Typical IT landscape of insurance companies (© SAP AG)

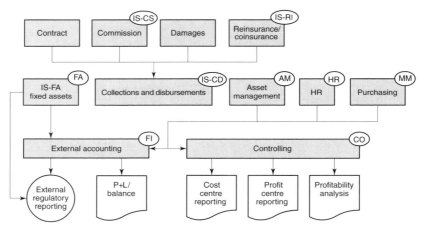

FIGURE 6.5   Reorganized value flow with mySAP Insurance (© SAP AG)

requirements of Swiss business law and the management's need for control. Legal requirements demanded that the companies within the group maintain and balance their legal regulations according to each industry. Management, however, wanted a multi-dimensional and uniform view oriented to strategic business units. Today, the SAP solution enables the company to map a contribution margin in 15 different dimensions.

Faster time-to-market

The absence of a central business partner and the existence of numerous sector systems means that many insurance companies lose a central view of their customers. Companies often carry several policy accounts for one customer, each of which requires invoicing documents. That approach is not only difficult for customers to understand, but also complicates the integration of transactions and a consolidated view of customers and their needs. When one of Europe's largest insurance companies decided to implement SAP, it wanted customers and their business relationships with the insurer to stand in the centre. It wanted a horizontal, rather than a vertical, view of customer accounts. The company regarded solutions for collections and disbursements as particularly important for customer relations. Faster information and data exchange between IS-CD and other systems increased the efficiency of internal procedures. As one director put it, 'our product development cycle used to take an average of two years. Today, depending on the risks, we need two to three months.'

References

Datamonitor Europe (Ed.) (1999) *Technology in European Insurance: The Convergence of IT and Business Strategy*

Gesamtverband der Deutschen Versicherungswirtschaft e.V. (Ed.) (1999) *Langfristtrends und Perspektiven der Versicherungswirtschaft*, Schriftenreihe des Ausschusses Volkswirtschaft: 22

Gesamtverband der Deutschen Versicherungswirtschaft e.V. (Ed.) (1999) *Statistisches Taschenbuch der Versicherungswirtschaft*

Morgan Stanley Dean Witter (Ed.) (1999) *The Internet and Financial Services*, Financial$ervices.com

mySAP Media Industry Solution

Dr Roland Bürkle and Manfred Gärtner, SAP AG

Few other industries are experiencing the massive change that is currently taking place in the media industry. Although, very recently print media ruled the market, by 2010, it is estimated that print media will comprise less than 50 per cent of the European market. The rest of the market will belong to electronic media, with digital, online media showing the strongest growth (*see* Fig. 7.1). Given the current technological changes and the rapid advance of the Internet, these predictions may certainly become reality.

7.1 CURRENT TRENDS AND NEW OPPORTUNITIES IN THE MEDIA INDUSTRY

Customer desires

Customers today present their changing information requirements to media companies in all business sectors. Characteristics of their requirements include the following:

- Personalization of content, according to the needs of individual customers
- Increased timeliness of information
- Availability of information any time and anywhere
- Targeted information research

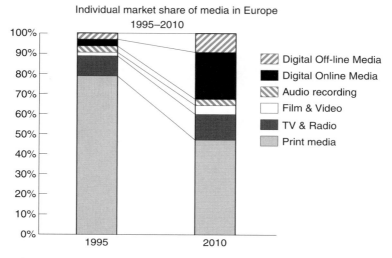

FIGURE 7.1 Share of individual media in the European media market (Diebold 1998) (© SAP AG)

■ Automatic, system-driven and timely delivery of the information required by any individual, enhanced by active information research (push information enhanced by pull information by e-mail or mobile phone)

■ Comprehensive information extended by interaction and the range of services and products on offer

■ Parallel use of different media for different purposes (print media, radio, TV, the Internet and so on)

Internet
The Internet plays a central role in this paradigm shift because it has enabled many customer requirements to be fulfilled for the first time. The Internet offers numerous new business opportunities, not only for relationships with customers, but also for those with partners, vendors, competitors, shareholders and, last but not least, employees (*see* Fig. 7.2).

Collaborative business processes
For example, for collaboration between partners and vendors, the Internet can handle business processes faster and more efficiently. Media companies can use the Internet to procure goods, services or the rights to use specific content, such as images, manuscripts, news, films or music. It also simplifies media production when authors may work in different countries. As long as the Internet is seamlessly integrated into the working environment, employees can use it as an additional source of information.

Three significant trends affect the competitive situation:

■ The Internet and the increasing digitalization of media products enable much simpler, more cost-effective and faster globalization, which leads to increased local competition

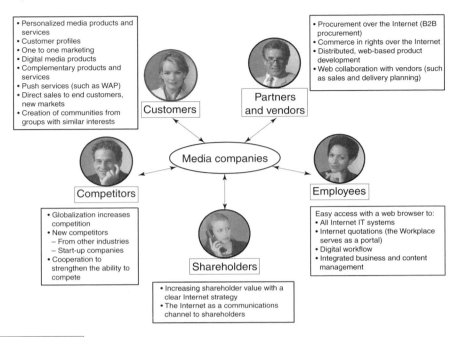

- Personalized media products and services
- Customer profiles
- One to one marketing
- Digital media products
- Complementary products and services
- Push services (such as WAP)
- Direct sales to end customers, new markets
- Creation of communities from groups with similar interests

Customers

Partners and vendors

- Procurement over the Internet (B2B procurement)
- Commerce in rights over the Internet
- Distributed, web-based product development
- Web collaboration with vendors (such as sales and delivery planning)

Media companies

Competitors

- Globalization increases competition
- New competitors
  – From other industries
  – Start-up companies
- Cooperation to strengthen the ability to compete

Employees

Easy access with a web browser to:
- All Internet IT systems
- Internet quotations (the Workplace serves as a portal)
- Digital workflow
- Integrated business and content management

Shareholders

- Increasing shareholder value with a clear Internet strategy
- The Internet as a communications channel to shareholders

FIGURE 7.2 Opportunities and challenges in the Internet economy (© SAP AG)

- Companies in other industries and dynamic start-up firms increasingly compete with established media companies. For example, newspapers can easily lose classified advertising to Internet companies offering jobs, cars or property on their websites. In the future, only a quick response to these challenges and an adequate business model can secure this important source of revenue for media companies

- Cooperation with other media companies, suppliers of complementary products and services and technology partners allow a comprehensive supply of information, products and services to secure a strong market position.

The precondition for taking advantage of these opportunities and strengthening competitive abilities in media companies is a high performance, Internet-enabled information technology, as offered by SAP.

| 7.2 | **THE SAP SOLUTION FOR MEDIA COMPANIES** |

Integrated solution

Today, hundreds of media companies successfully use standard SAP R/3. Typical back-office solutions, such as Financials, Controlling, Human Resources or Purchasing, originally played an important role. At the beginning of the 1990s, however, SAP began to enhance its industry-neutral applications with industry-specific components to offer media companies a comprehensive, integrated solution for all business processes. The focus of development lay in front-office solutions for the distribution of newspapers and magazines via subscriptions and direct sales, classified advertising in print and online media, and advertising on radio and TV. Open interfaces for the easily accessible integration of technical production systems, such as preprint solutions in print media or banner management systems for online advertising, complete mySAP Media. As well as the development of additional functional modules, the solution focuses on the integrated use of the Internet for business processes in media companies.

Best practices

SAP supports the implementation of software solutions in media companies with best practice procedures and the appropriate tools for the job. For example, it provides a procedure model for implementation, a question catalogue for ascertaining requirements, and media-specific defaults for processes. SAP partners also offer additional support that includes preconfigured solutions for both small and medium-sized media companies.

7.2.1 Media Solution Map

Solution Map

The Media Solution Map (Table 7.1) gives an overview of the essential business processes in media companies and shows how mySAP media supports them.

If a media company operates in only one part of the business area, it uses only those processes shown for that part.

Financial processes

Whereas the middle levels of the Solution Map depict core logistical processes, the upper level primarily describes financial processes: internal accounting, external accounting and strategic planning. It also describes SAP Business Information Warehouse, which acts as a central tool for the collection, summarizing and evaluation of company and market data, and provides the basis for numerous other activities, from database marketing to defining key performance indicators.

Staging processes

The two lower levels describe the processes for preparing business-oriented production factors. These levels show media assets in more detail because of their importance to media companies. In addition to simply managing media assets, these features link the assets to the corresponding documents (content objects) and rights for any media objects, including procuring objects with licences and licence settlement.

Product publication

The remaining levels represent core logistical processes that include product development, subsequent publishing of the developed product by printing, transmission or online publishing. They also illustrate Customer Relationship Management for the types of products produced in media companies:

- Digital and non-digital media products (books, magazines, films, CDs and TV programmes)

- Advertising services (textual and designed advertisements, online advertisements and advertising spots)

- Licenses for media assets

TABLE 7.1   Media Solution Map

Enterprise Management	Strategic Enterprise Management	Business Intelligence	Managerial Accounting	Financial Accounting	Sales Management
Customer Relationship Management	Customer Service	Market Research & Analysis	Product/ Brand Marketing	Marketing Programme Management	
Production	Media Content Planning	Media Production Planning	Media Production Controlling	Metal Object Editing	Composing	Activity Recording
Publication	Publication Planning	Printing	Broadcasting	Online Publishing	CD ROM Manufacturing
Sales Cycle Management Advertising	Business Partner Management	Sales Order Management	Billing/ Invoicing	Contract Management	Settlements
Sales Cycle Management Media Products	Business Partner Management	Sales Order Management	Logistic Execution	Billing/ Invoicing	Settlements
Sales Cycle Management Licenses	Business Partner Management	Sales Order Management	Billing/ Invoicing	Contract Management	Settlements
Media Asset Management	Media Asset Procurement	Content Management	Rights Management	Royalty Accounting	
Business Support	Human Resource Core Functions & Strategy	Human Resource Analytics & Enabling Solutions	Procurement	Treasury/ Corporate Finance Management	Fixed Asset Management	Equipment Maintenance

Customer
Relationship
Management

The aim of Customer Relationship Management is to represent the entire customer life cycle from marketing to distribution to service (*see* Fig. 7.3). It should offer integrated support for all product types, all communications channels with customers (Internet, telephone, field sales and written documents), and all distribution channels (retail and direct distribution). This level of integration enables a unified overview of customers. As is true of all SAP solutions, *my*SAP Customer Relationship Management is linked to other components to offer comprehensive support for business processes, for example to back-office systems for order fulfilment (delivery and invoicing), or to planning components to check product availability.

For more detailed information and current availability status of the actual functions behind the process modules, please visit www.sap.com.

7.2.2 A Typical Business Case

Subscription
management

The following uses subscription management at a regional newspaper as an example of a typical business case. On the one hand, the example can present the interplay between individual organizational units of the publisher and the support of the overall process by SAP by mapping the real world in a completely integrated software system. On the other hand, it shows the opportunities offered by the use of the Internet in a publisher's traditional business process. Numerous customers in international publishing use the functions of *my*SAP Media described here for subscription management of newspapers and magazines.

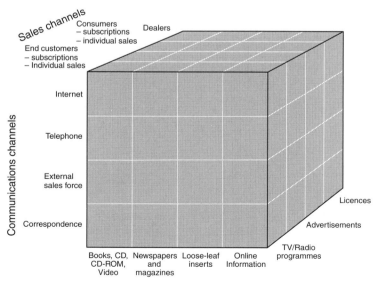

FIGURE 7.3   Cross-media/cross-product Customer Relationship Management (© SAP AG)

Customer life cycle

As shown in Fig. 7.4 mySAP Media covers the entire customer life cycle: initial customer acquisition, subscription maintenance and long-term customer relationship management. mySAP Media supplies all the relevant information to all the organizational units of a publisher or its partners, and integrates all software components with an orientation to the process involved.

Advertising campaign: offering phase

mySAP Media supports the processes involved in advertising for subscribers. After you define the type of advertising you need, you then select a target group from a database of addresses and send out an advertising flyer. In many cases, and when permitted by law, companies can bypass the postal service and have a newspaper delivery service deliver the flyer to non-subscribers. mySAP Media stores the list of addresses used in the campaign, so you can later determine its effectiveness by comparing the original target group with the resulting list of subscribers.

Subscription orders

The recipient decides to subscribe for a given period. In the example above, the addressee might fill out the coupon included with the flyer and post it to the publisher. The new subscriber can also select a subscription bonus, such as a discount or free gift.

Addressees can also subscribe by contacting the publisher's call centre. Increasingly, new subscribers choose to order directly from the publisher's website, thus placing an order at any time and from any location.

Regardless of the communications channel chosen by the new subscriber, their order must be entered quickly and securely. mySAP Media supports the acceptance of orders with numerous automatic features and checks the following:

- The new subscriber's address is checked against a country-specific list of postal codes and street lists; the system completes any missing information

- Depending upon the type of delivery (direct or through the postal service), the system suggests the next edition that can be delivered

- Depending upon the type of subscription and the desired form and means of payment, the customer receives a quotation immediately

Order processing and related processes

Acceptance of a subscription order triggers a variety of activities at the publisher and its partners. These generally remain invisible to readers. Readers have only one concern:

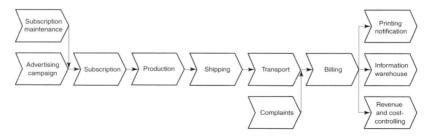

FIGURE 7.4 The Subscription Management process (© SAP AG)

that the paper arrives on time so that they can read it when they want to. mySAP Media ensures that this takes place.

Creating a subscription order triggers the following activities:

- The order is assigned to the appropriate advertising campaign; the subscription bonus is sent to the new subscriber

- Subscription accounting is informed of the order; the system handles invoicing according to the desired payment method and sends a bill in a timely manner

- The next shipment includes a copy for the new subscriber; the delivery service receives information about the new customer

- The customer receives a welcome letter and a service brochure that includes information about additional services offered by the publisher, such as reader tours or concerts

- Subscription statistics are updated; previously calculated press runs for future editions are updated in seconds

Subscription maintenance

The life cycle of a subscription includes various types of changes and frequently involves dealing with exceptions. mySAP Media supports both kinds of activities with equal speed and quality in the logistical process. Examples here include suspended delivery due to holiday or illness and redirecting delivery to an alternative location.

In such cases, customers can inform the publisher that they want the service to change by means of various communications channels: by letter, coupon, fax, telephone, the Internet or personal visit to a branch location. Subscription maintenance also involves handling complaints, and long-term customer retention.

Complaints

Logistical problems can sometimes cause late delivery or non-delivery. When a customer reports such an event, the publisher starts trying to solve the problem as quickly as possible and to the customer's satisfaction. All the other organizational units involved receive information about the problem in seconds to trigger immediate redelivery. Other customers in the same delivery area who have also complained about non-delivery can be informed of the steps already taken to solve the problem.

Customer retention

To retain their customers in the long term, media companies must remind subscribers when their subscriptions are about to expire and make a new offer that invites renewal. Once a customer renews a subscription, the customer relationship life cycle closes.

Reporting and analysis

Special statistics that show adherence to contracts or differentiate printing runs also belong to the functional scope of mySAP Media. The company-wide SAP Business Information Warehouse contains all the numbers and evaluations needed for internal decision-making as well as external statistics, for example relating to national and international company associations in the publishing field.

New offerings

In addition to newspaper or magazine subscriptions, publishers increasingly offer other subscription-like contracts, such as those for online access to information databases. These developments increase the need for integrated solutions for media asset management, digital availability, the delivery of information and the extensive use of the Internet. The SAP Media solution already integrates the required components.

7.2.3 Additional Development: mySAP.com for Media Companies

mySAP.com

To respond to the requirements and opportunities of the new Internet economy, mySAP.com has redeveloped these fundemental components:

- The Workplace as an employee's portal
- The Marketplace as a location for communications, information, e-commerce and e-collaboration
- E-business scenarios for media companies
- Application hosting

It also includes several enhancements for all the functional areas shown in the Solution Map. The enhancements significantly improve handling of the system (EnjoySAP Initiative), expand existing functions and make available new functions.

mySAP Workplace

Personal Workplace

mySAP Workplace was developed to offer every employee in a media company a tailor-made work environment. The Workplace not only offers access to role-based SAP functions, but also enables employees to access the functions of non-SAP systems and Internet offerings (news, rights, services and so on) from a standard user interface.

Role model

The configuration of a web browser includes a menu that depends upon the user's role and includes any required functions. The drag-and-drop function can be used to easily link individual functions to other functions that apply to the same object, such as an order, a customer, a delivery note and so on.

The work-oriented organizational structure of a model media company provides the basis for the roles contained in mySAP Media. Concrete SAP functions are then assigned to the role. Typical roles include a sales director, sales clerk, field sales representative, advertising director, financial accountant, controller and personnel clerk. The roles delivered by SAP merely act as a template for simpler and faster definitions of company-specific roles that are to be tailored to each organization.

Once a user has successfully logged on to the system, the Workplace features another important function. It automatically displays the information most important to the user: sales figures, customer complaints, incoming e-mail, stock prices and so on. Users can redesign this interface to best meet their own personal needs.

Marketplace

The mySAP.com Marketplace offers both general business information and functions and media-specific information such as innovations and trends in the industry, meetings,

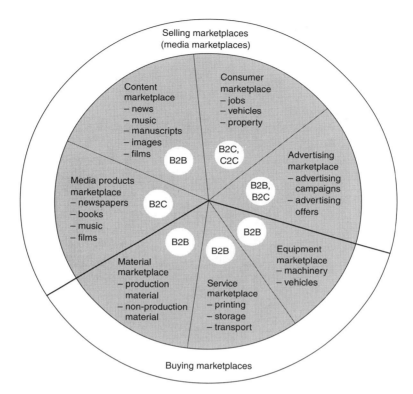

FIGURE 7.5   Possible marketplaces for media companies (© SAP AG)

organizations and discussion forums. In addition to this general marketplace, other, more specialized marketplaces can also be designed (*see* Fig. 7.5). For the media industry, marketplaces can focus on the following:

- Business with media assets
- Sales of advertising services
- Sales of media products
- Car, job, or property advertisements in addition to classified advertising

In general, the Marketplace can also be used for marketplaces that are not operated by SAP itself.

E-Business Scenarios for Media Companies

E-business scenarios (or Internet business scenarios) use the Internet to optimize business processes in media companies. An examination of the network within which media companies operate gives the following overview (*see* Fig. 7.6):

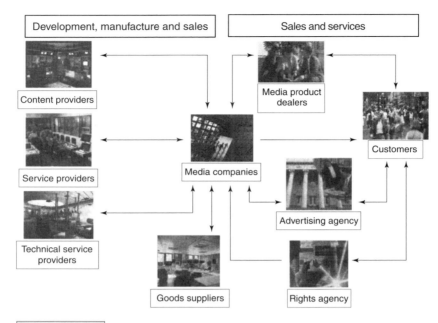

FIGURE 7.6 The media world: a global network of specialists (© SAP AG)

E-business scenarios include both the optimization of business processes with end customers (e-commerce) and collaboration with retailers, agents, or vendors (e-collaboration).

Internet sales of classified advertising
Internet product sales

An example of an e-commerce scenario is the sale of classified advertising or advertisements over the Internet (*see* Fig. 7.7).

The Internet already supports the online sale of subscriptions to newspapers and magazines and maintenance of these subscriptions (suspended deliveries, redirection during holidays, and changing addresses for customers). Using the Internet to deliver digital products, such as music or specific information, also offers interesting opportunities. The significance of the world wide web will continue to increase through technologies such as e-books (electronic books) and may become serious competition for classical media in some areas. SAP is currently developing solutions in this area.

Collaboration scenarios

SAP also plans solutions for collaboration scenarios which include the following:

▨ Sales of advertising that involves the client, advertising agency and media company

▨ Planning delivery quantities with media companies and retailers

▨ Development of a new book that includes authors from around the world

Such collaboration scenarios involve significant potential for optimizing business processes to the benefit of all those involved.

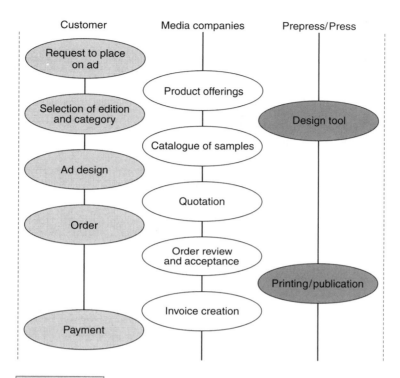

FIGURE 7.7   Internet sales of advertising (© SAP AG)

7.3   TWO SAMPLE APPLICATIONS

7.3.1 A Regional Newspaper Publisher

New strategic
directions with
integrated
advertising
management

A large regional newspaper in Germany uses the SAP Advertising Management System, IS-M/AM, as well as other SAP components. The publisher offers local newspapers, weekly reviews, special interest newspapers and heavily visited online publications. The publisher also handles radio and TV schedules.

The company wants to be able to handle all the business processes in advertising management in a uniform manner using a completely integrated commercial solution that includes the seamless integration of the required technical services, such as the production of advertising in the pre-press environment.

At the beginning of system implementation, the publisher defined its strategic goal as being to provide optimum support for their decentralized but uniform procedure processing system. In addition to IS-M/AM, it implemented a new system landscape for newspaper and advertising production and integrated it with the existing open communication interfaces of IS-M/AM. This integration, implemented for the first time in such a wide range of applications, gave the publisher new perspectives on process optimization.

The entire process chain was redefined to link all steps from the acquisition of advertising orders to camera-ready copy (CRC). Since the start of production in July 1998, IS-M/AM has controlled all the processes related to the acquisition and settlement of advertising services according to individual publisher and customer regulations. The acquisition of new advertising customers is also supported, along with contract closing and order processing. The publisher also saw IS-M/AM as the key to designing completely new, integrated processes.

An example clarifies this development. Previously, an advertising order was accepted by the advertising department and sent to the art department to be designed. IS-M/AM integrates the design function (advertisement editor) into the overall procedure and makes it possible to process the advertising order in one step, in one department. Doing so guarantees quick order throughput, fewer errors and uniform customer management. The management has made the following evaluation of the new system landscape. One member of the management team said, 'We can now handle our business processes in a transparent and integrated manner. Decentralized, uniform processing places more responsibility on employees, accelerates processing and increases the quality of the business processes.'

7.3.2 A Modern Television Company

Optimizing the logistics chain for purchasing film and licences

A media company with new, modern television products and television-related markets such as merchandising, multimedia and studio production uses SAP Media to plan, manage and control general business and media-specific business processes. By implementing the system, the company optimized the entire logistics chain for purchasing film and licences.

Accounting has recognized the positive effects of the system. For example, SAP Media has significantly increased the transparency of internal and external reporting. The ability to access the company-wide, uniform database directly has also optimized the availability of information at all levels of the company. The high level of integration among the applications has enabled the company to accelerate its processes and increase its overall productivity.

Users found integrated processing of film stock (including inventory management), financial accounting and depreciation policies particularly beneficial. SAP Media has effected a long-term increase in efficiency throughout the entire logistics chain for the purchase of film and licences.

After implementing the system, the company stated, 'Integrated processing in connection with simultaneous optimization of industry-specific business processes lets us comfortably meet the increased demands placed upon public companies by the new legal requirements.'

mySAP Mill Products Industry Solution for the Metal, Paper and Textile Industries

Daniel Stimson and Reinhild Gefrerer
SAP AG

8.1 A UNIFIED INDUSTRY?

Industries and IT

SAP's many years of development and effort have shown that preparing standard software for the metal, wood/paper and textile industries is a daunting task. Leif Eriksen (1999) described the reason for the difficulty very clearly: 'When touring these plants, you get the impression that you're visiting several different operations.'

Common features in the metal, paper and textile industries

Just what do you understand by mill products? This is often the central question in conversations about the SAP Industry Solution. Although the English term includes textile mills, steel mills or paper mills, hardly any other languages have a term such as 'mill' that can apply across the board to these manufacturers and to a series of other industries as well.

Worldwide, the mill products industry produces goods valued at $1.5 billion annually. It ranks sixth among the twenty Industry Business Units (IBUs) classified by SAP. Some of its branches form complete logistics chains, from mining to metal production, for example. In other branches, however, mill products represent only a partial step in the value-added chain. For example, the production of textiles is clearly different to the sale and distribution of clothing. Accordingly, the question arises as to which features these different sectors have in common.

Multilevel production

Common features exist at the highest production level in the form of comparable manufacturing and logistics processes. In these industries, production usually takes place in several steps (multilevel production). Production involves a procedure that stands between discrete production and process manufacturing. Another term used in this context is multi-modal production. Closer examination quickly reveals the defining characteristics in the planning and production procedures of this type of industry.

Product
characteristics

It is as hard to summarize the manufacturers of 'mill products' as it is to describe the products they produce. A single product, such as a metal bar or a large roll of paper, can undergo further processing to become a wide variety of end products, such as sheet metal or various kinds of paper. Frequently, although not always, the production process involves a variant of make-to-order production. The more that a product takes on a specific form during production, a form that continues to change, the stronger the need is for differentiated characteristics to describe it, including quality, type, colour, size and so on. For various reasons, however, the end product does not always display the planned characteristics. This issue becomes more critical depending upon how much the manufacturing process follows the conditions of make-to-order production, and often requires replanning or reworking.

Stagnating profit
margins

Globalization and domestic competition have drastically affected profit margins in the metal, paper and textile industries. Customers in these industries usually have a technical advantage and give the final recipient of products a great deal of control options. To regain lost ground, many manufacturers attempt to improve their influence and revenues through mergers and takeovers. These attempts result in consolidation of the market without forcing any increase in productivity or profitability.

High use of
capital

▨ Manufacturers

Companies in the metal, paper and textile industries are essentially capital-intensive. To maximize the use of assets, production in these industries takes the form of continuous production processes. Plant managers consistently strive for the highest possible production yield. Performance indicators, such as 'tonnes produced in each unit of time' are the rule. In the past, setting these goals has led to paying less attention to cost and quality control. This has recently changed, however, and now increasingly profitability of production is included as a decisive performance criterion. In some cases, maximum profitability occurs even before the production assets run with a full load.

Higher product
quality

▨ Dealers

Metal and wholesale paper dealers are independent companies that handle distribution for manufacturers. They deliver semi-finished goods, components and material from affiliated companies. These deliveries create new forms of collaboration that also demand the development of products with higher added value.

8.1.1 New, Industry-Wide Thinking About E-Commerce and the Internet

According to recent studies, the metal, paper and textile industries have come to regard the triumphal march of the Internet and e-commerce as unstoppable (*see* Niittymäki 1999). Early proponents have already formulated appropriate business strategies, and the general stance in the industry has changed from waiting to action. Accordingly, questions usually do not address what to do, but focus on the search for appropriate measures.

Customers as the driving force in e-commerce

First studies have already been undertaken by the industry on the readiness and ability of its customers to participate in e-commerce. They indicate that individual customer groups (such as publishers in the paper industry) are more involved with the development and opportunities of e-commerce than other groups. Some groups appear more open to e-commerce and cooperation over the Internet than the manufacturers themselves. These groups act as the driving force behind current development.

Tuning e-commerce to industry-specific requirements is an extremely demanding task. Some consultants and suppliers who specialize in e-commerce believe that the same characteristics and conditions apply to all branches of the economy. They are wrong. Particularly in the metal, paper and textile industries, industry-specific requirements can significantly limit the use of the basic principles of e-commerce.

8.1.2 Mill Products and the Internet

Numerous factors come into play when evaluating Internet technologies in the metal, paper and textile industries. Each sector must weigh the factors differently, in the light of its own needs.

Production Capacity and Market Share

An enormous potential for revenue counts among the most frequently mentioned and principal advantages of e-commerce. In the metal, paper and textile industries, however, individual production capacity is generally limited to the short-term market share that a company can achieve. The limitation applies to any resource-dependent sector of the economy. For e-commerce, the question then arises of how to get the maximum revenues from the existing capacity at the lowest possible price. Against this background, it becomes clear that e-commerce scenarios in these industries must first involve more intense collaboration with large customers. Companies can reach this goal by supporting and improving the business practices common to the industry.

Changed thinking in order processing

In addition, e-commerce requires a redistribution of responsibilities in order processing. Capacity management plays a key role in the metal, paper and textile industries. Production managers currently have responsibility for the optimum use of production assets. In the view of order processing in e-commerce, however, process sovereignty should belong to customer service or to sales and distribution. In other words, customer demand, not asset load, should determine processing. Companies must change the ways they think, and they certainly cannot do this overnight.

Transportation Costs

Global
processing,
regional
production

At the first levels of production, mill products usually have relatively little value. Accordingly, transportation costs become an important factor: a production site can serve only a limited geographical area. Outside this region, transportation costs become so high that delivery is unprofitable. Despite the lack of borders on the Internet, sales made in e-commerce scenarios can only occur regionally. When deciding which plant will fulfil the demand of an individual customer, companies must consider profitability as an important criterion. The software used in this area must respect this requirement.

Potential customers who search for a supplier on the Internet must also consider regions as a principal criterion. Although customers can theoretically look at products that are available all over the world, it makes more sense for them to request quotations only from companies who can provide cost-effective delivery.

Different Markets, Different Strategies

Sales in the metal, paper and textile industries by internal sales personnel are usually desirable because this process step adds more value. Regional differences exist here. Companies in the US, for example, place more emphasis on efficient sales processing than do European companies. The development of an e-commerce strategy must consider these differences.

The scenario chosen for e-commerce must orient itself to the requirements of the target market. For example, the idea of a virtual marketplace is better suited to sales of production overruns in foreign markets than to primary sales.

Any e-commerce strategy in the metal, paper and textile industries must also consider the significant differences between individual product groups. Such differences include the sales organization, the value added, the number and variety of sales transactions, and the size of the sales markets. They also involve a spectrum of basic products, customer-specific goods, make-to-order products and semi-finished goods. Even the specifications for individual product characteristics can differ in each target market. E-commerce solutions must therefore vary as much as the effects of e-commerce on product groups. They must deal with each product group individually and specifically.

Effects on the Value-Added Chain

The rise in popularity of e-commerce has put pressure on traditional sales structures. However, a general detour around traditional distribution channels is not necessarily the goal of e-commerce (Fig. 8.1).

Large customers who are still covered by wholesale and retail sales already demand the opportunity to buy directly from the manufacturer. E-commerce will increase this pressure. Traditional retailers remain an important link between smaller and private end customers, and are an important partner and customer of manufacturers.

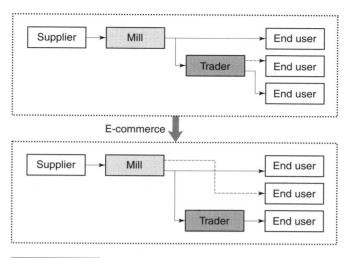

E-commerce in the metal, paper and textile industries: motivation and roadblocks

The primary motivating factors for implementing e-commerce in the metal, paper and textile industries include competitive pressure, the demand for better service available around the clock and economic pressures. One central aspect involves the use of the Internet to improve customer service without high costs. This approach first requires an analysis of the business relationships between suppliers and customers as well as an examination of the possibilities available to tighten the relevant transactions (sales). Leaders in this area will have a clear lead. Some companies consider direct sales over the Internet to be a reason for launching an e-commerce venture. Surprisingly, what appears to be a main argument in other industries, the ability to reach a worldwide group of customers, does not play a special role for suppliers of mill products.

According to manufacturers, the greatest roadblocks on the way to e-commerce include a lack of detailed project plans, the existing technical infrastructure, negative experiences with IT and the risk involved with price-oriented purchasing decisions. Companies also ask how customers can be encouraged to use online services.

The primary interests of those who purchase mill products seem to include efficient purchasing, improved self-service and release from activities that do not involve their core business. The introduction of stock carried by vendors can reach these goals. Customers also expect cross-company planning to lower capital costs and prices.

From a customer's viewpoint, the number of online systems with which they must deal hinders e-commerce. If the supplier and customer systems are not linked, the work involved for customers doubles. They must enter their orders in the supplier's online system and then re-enter it into their own order entry systems. In this instance, an e-commerce scenario, such as a virtual marketplace, can offer distinct advantages.

No one can deny the revolutionary effects information technology has had on the modern economy. The Internet particularly demands quick strategic decisions from companies. Anyone who wishes to conduct business in the future must react at Internet speed. An Internet year corresponds to about 60 days of conventional time.

Is speed everything in the age of the world wide web? Absolutely not. Think of the effort involved in establishing a virtual marketplace for the metalworking industry. Several players entered this area early but have since left it because they accomplished too little and saw no significant profits in sight – at least in the first few years of operation. According to a recent US poll, 31 per cent of customers have expressed an interest in buying metal products over the Internet. However, only 6 per cent of customers actually make purchases over the Internet (*see* Brunelli 1999).

Silo principle versus Internet Business Framework

The situation doesn't look much different for business application software, which includes the Internet. Particularly in the metal, paper and textile industries, many software companies follow the silo principle. They specialize in individual industries or functional areas and then use this foundation to expand the functional scope of their products. SAP has chosen another path. Beginning with a high-performance, open and flexible basic architecture, the Internet Business Framework, SAP has developed industry-specific functions in close collaboration with its customers and partners. The result is a multi-faceted software package that covers a wide spectrum of processes, built on a solid technical foundation.

SAP has always regarded the metal, paper and textile industries as strategically important. As partners, these industries have co-developed mySAP Mill Products and mySAP Supply Chain Management (mySAP SCM), the logistics solution driven by mySAP.com. More than 2,000 producers of mill products already use SAP solutions to control their production processes.

Use of SAP software for the metal, paper and textile industries

How does SAP respond to the needs of this sector? The mySAP Mill Products Industry Solution offers a technical infrastructure for integration and performance optimization along the entire logistics chain.

The development of the software for the Mill Products Industry Solution began in 1995 (Table 8.1). A specific project team mapped the business processes for the metal processing industry (steel, aluminium and casting), the paper industry and the textile industry. The project focused on processes in planning, production, inventory management, quality assurance, costing and sales.

mySAP Mill Products incorporates SAP's many years of experience in the industry. The software directs the requirements of the metal, paper and textile industries to SAP service and product development. The employees of the IBU for metal, paper and wood products have a decisive influence on the design of mySAP.com solutions for logistics processes. SAP enjoys the support of numerous partners.

Special solutions for wire and cable manufacturers

One result of the close collaboration of SAP and its customers is the SAP Cable Solution, developed in 1992. This offers an Industry Solution which can be used

TABLE 8.1 Mill Products Solution Map

Enterprise Management	Strategic Enterprise Management	Business Intelligence	Managerial Accounting	Financial Accounting	Sales Management
Customer Relationship Management	Customer Service	Market Research & Analysis	Product/Brand Marketing	Marketing Programme Management	
Product & Process Engineering	Environmental Health & Safety	Plant Maintenance	Quality Management	Product Development	
Data Management & Engineering Change Management	Master Data Management	Product Data Management	Customer/Material Data Management	Master Data & Document Change Management	
Sales	Demand Planning	Sales Order Clarification	Order Acknowledgement & Maintenance	Sales Cycle Management	
Raw Material & Resource Management	Procurement Planning	Raw Material Purchasing	Raw Material Transportation	Inventory Management	Quality Inspection
Process Manufacturing	Process Scheduling & Planning	Production Execution	Process Control	Quality Control	
Manufacturing/ Conversion	Inventory Management	Production Planning	Production Execution	Outside Processing	
Distribution	Logistics Planning	Shipping	Transportation	Storage & Site Management	Warehouse Management
Business Support	Human Resource Core Functions & Strategy	Human Resource Analytics & Enabling Solutions	Procurement	Treasury	Fixed Asset Management

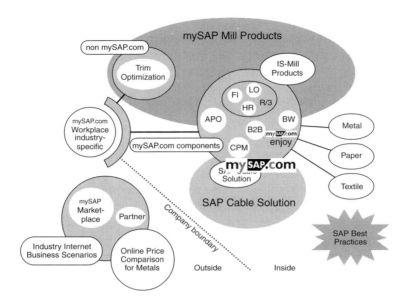

FIGURE 8.2 Software solutions from the IBU for metal, paper and wood products
(© SAP AG)

internationally. Although the business processes in the cable industry share some similarities with those of mill products companies, the SAP Cable Solution is best suited for the manufacture of high tension, fibre optic or telecommunications cable (Fig. 8.2).

Better information through data integration

The most important performance characteristics of mySAP Mill Products include the linking of logistics, planning and production to external and internal accounting. This link takes special, industry-specific factors, primarily product specifications and technical production requirements, into consideration. As a rule, mill products deal with production variants that are planned and manufactured in the context of multilevel make-to-order production according to the customer order.

The applications in mySAP Mill Products support the entire logistics chain: from product specification and configuration, to rough planning and order processing, and to capacity planning and production. They include costing, inventory management, quality assurance and, along with costing, integration with accounting and cost accounting. The following offers an overview of some applications.

Product specification with variants

The possible number of product characteristics and variants presents special challenges to IT in the metal, paper and textile industries. The customer order lists the required characteristics that are to be created in several production steps. During this process, hundreds of characteristics might be added, which requires the processing of a huge amount of data. mySAP Mill Products use an integrated variant configurator to predefine product groups, classes and characteristics for two purposes: to limit the data that requires processing, and to allow additional variants.

Configurable material masters are created for each product group or incoming product group and are assigned to a variant class. These master records are used later on by order processing, production and inventory management. During production the products undergo linked production steps, such as rolling, heating, cutting, layering or plating. SAP R/3 makes it possible to create specific master records for products at each production level. The feature increases transparency and simplifies the processing of intermediate orders for planning. Material lists link individual production steps and contain entries about the starting materials, quantities required and planned scrap for each step.

Order processing

Customer order processing plays a central role in variant production for material planning, capacity planning and production. When an order is received, the required product characteristics and other relevant data (delivery data, conditions and so on) are first created. Customer-specific check criteria and delivery conditions play an important role here. To simplify the entry of large volumes of data, mySAP Mill Products can combine these criteria and conditions for individual customers and store them in tables. Product characteristics also help to determine the selling price.

To enable later changes to the order data, mySAP Mill Products can store new information that derives from order entry or appears after the start of production separately, without overwriting the output data. The MRP controller can display the progress of planning and production in hierarchical status reports and then use this information to release or reject changes to the customer order.

Production planning and material planning

The process chain in mySAP Mill Products automatically redirects order items to requirements planning. All the production steps are pre-planned and the required external or internal procurement measures are triggered here. Using the order volume, the system calculates the necessary raw materials and uses planning orders to create a schedule for all production steps. The planning order contains the quantities of incoming goods, start dates, finish dates and all the raw materials in use.

Order confirmation with availability check

SAP Advanced Planner & Optimizer (SAP APO) enhances the functions of mySAP Mill Products. Industry sectors that use make-to-order production require interactive availability checks during order entry. The availability check provides the employee with responsibility for this with all the information needed to confirm incoming orders.

The functional scope of the availability check includes:

- Multilevel check on the availability of the required materials
- Multilevel, cross-plant capacity check

Production planning with SAP APO

The mature planning procedures in SAP APO include a comprehensive range of tools for processing distribution, sales, transportation and production planning. Detailed planning tunes logistics to the requirements determined by forecast calculation. It does so by using the appropriate algorithms together with optimized decision-making processes, response processes and selecting sources across plants.

Coordinating requirements

SAP APO can also combine various raw materials requirements for an individual production run. The source indication from SAP APO coordinates the planning requirements of several orders and is used to maintain the data of the original order throughout the individual production steps.

Production control

The next step in the process chain involves production control. Before production starts, the planning orders are selected and converted into production orders. The production orders contain all the information required on product configuration, schedules, quantities, work plans and raw materials used. Because the metal, paper and textile industries usually work with multilevel production procedures, mySAP Mill Products makes it possible to link the order to individual steps. The production order describes the steps and links them to subsequent steps. This feature makes it possible to plan all the production steps for the entire group. To support coordinated processing of these steps, mySAP Mill Products groups production orders from various sources by combining orders. It also lets you split orders into individual production lots at a later point if any deviations occur in raw materials substitutions or production processes.

The certified production control systems that are integrated into SAP R/3 over standard interfaces can automatically record confirmations and raw material movements for scrap and remainders.

SAP PP-PI (Production Planning for the Process Industry) ensures seamless information exchange between mySAP Mill Products and process control. The entry of specific process characteristics makes it possible to tune the input and output data of individual production steps to operational needs. This feature enables you to capture all the relevant process data (temperature, speed, pressure and so on) and product data (type, measurements, size, etc.).

Cost accounting

Cost accounting in mySAP Mill Products supports ongoing, up-to-date and daily monitoring, updating and settlement of costs and revenues. It provides a comprehensive planning and control instrument for synchronizing the contents and flows of business processes. It can plan costs and revenue across several areas and monitor them closely. It recognizes deviations between planned and actual costs early on, leaving you enough leeway for corrective measures. A uniform reporting system delivers a solid information basis for planning and operative decisions, organized according to cost types and cost centres. It supports all commonly used cost accounting methods, from absorption costing to process cost accounting.

Order revenues and actual costs flow into profitability analysis and other analytical procedures. By evaluating customer, material and product data (such as steel grades, measurements and so on), these procedures provide comprehensive information to support planning decisions.

Quality assurance

Integrated quality assurance functions simplify the planning, monitoring and control of production quality. mySAP Mill Products manages QA (quality assurance) documents and technical drawings, prevents the delivery of low-quality goods, monitors problem processing and optimizes inspection operations with efficient sampling. Inspection lots (quality inspection orders) can be generated from production scrap or partial quantities of production orders. This function includes inspection processing, the generation of results and the formulation of usage decisions. Individual and multiple inspection lots can be created for every production lot. The inspection characteristics are copied directly from the production order into the inspection lot.

Once the results have been entered, you can re-access the characteristics analysis at any time.

Inventory management

Inventory is divided into different types: available stock, quality stock, reserved stock and so on. You can also sort by customer order, and the system supports stock transfers (cancellations or restocking) between individual orders. mySAP Mill Products accepts the entry of quantities in several types of measurement: not only in inventory management, but also in distribution, planning and production.

Monitoring of a material

Partial stock is managed at the batch level in inventory management. A flexible system handles batch determination, a system that selects material components based upon batch characteristics. Monitoring of raw materials produces an extensive and complete where-used list. Special functions, developed specifically for SAP Mill Products, can store a proof of origin in a batch log. This feature enables direct access to the analysis data of all the products in a specific production run.

Shipping and invoicing

The process chain handled by mySAP Mill Products ends with the delivery and invoicing of a product. It supports third-party delivery, delivery with interim storage and consignment (a business form in which the supplier places goods at a customer location without receiving payment until after sale or use of the goods). Invoicing calculates order item and transport costs and sends invoices to the accounting department.

Financial accounting

Financial Accounting includes all billing-relevant transactions, provides a seamless audit trail, and serves as an orientation aid for business planning and controlling tasks. The applications in this area apply to companies of all sizes, including large, multinational groups. Data from individual documents act as the basis for postings that the system then generates, checks and synchronously updates during integrated processing of a business transaction. In addition, Financial Accounting covers all the requirements of asset management. Integrated investment management allows the posting, planning and monitoring of capital investments. You can also link the processing of plant management activities directly to asset accounting.

8.2.1 The SAP Best Practice Initiative

In the context of its Best Practice Initiative, SAP offers its customers preconfigured systems that are oriented to the material, resource and processing needs of individual industries. This initiative aims to accelerate SAP implementation projects and quickly introduce customers to the mapping of industry-specific tasks in mySAP Mill Products.

In collaboration with industry experts from partner companies, the IBU for metal, paper and wood products currently offers the following scenarios:

- SAP Best Practice for the metalworking industry
- SAP Best Practice for the paper industry
- SAP Best Practice for textile production

Based upon the best practices mapped by SAP, several SAP customers from the metal, paper and textile industries have already formulated goals for their implementation projects. SAP Best Practices for the metalworking industry offers industry-specific business processes such as characteristic-dependent price determination, scrap processing and quality inspections. The use of SAP Best Business Practices also provides significant transfer of knowledge. SAP Best Practice can be used immediately and is delivered with comprehensive process documentation. Users can work productively with the system from the very first day. According to SAP customers, the use of SAP Best Practice saves over 30 per cent of the costs of traditional implementation projects.

8.2.2 mySAP.com for the Metal, Paper and Textile Industries

The effects of the Internet on logistics in the metal, paper and textile industries and mySAP.com also apply to the Metal, Paper and Wood Products IBU. Along with SAP, forward-looking companies from these industries define the special needs of the industry and study the applicability of SAP products.

Maximizing the efficiency of order processing, consistently delivering the correct quantity and quality at the agreed date, and operating at the lowest possible cost all require integrated planning, timely control, an event-triggered ordering process and current inventory data from all production areas. The currently used IT systems provide the following:

▓ Increased transparency of integrated manufacturing processes

▓ Improved productivity and reduced costs

▓ Optimized load on production equipment

▓ Simplified fulfilment of customers' demands for quality

▓ Availability at any time of planned/actual comparisons for quality, time and cost

By accessing SAP R/3 and specialized transport and warehouse materials planning, mySAP.com optimizes logistics processing. Across the company, employees with key functions or newly-defined business roles (such as an e-business expert or a logistics coordinator) access all the information they need to perform their jobs. Based upon industry-specific key figures, SAP customers who have implemented the SAP logistics solution have already been able to achieve revenue increases up to 166 per cent. Business advantages also await these industries.

SAP logistics processing occurs over portals to the mySAP Workplace. The portals can be personalized, are role-specific and are oriented toward other employees and to customers. Role-specific portals are available for customers, end consumers, employees and suppliers. Logistics processing over the mySAP Marketplace can also be linked to the logistics solutions of other suppliers.

As an industry-specific portal, the mySAP Marketplace bundles all the market information required by manufacturers of mill products. Special offers for distribution, product information and market analysis along with customer and vendor profiles simplify day-to-day work. SAP is the only manufacturer that already delivers software solutions for cross-company cooperation that can be personalized.

8.2.3 mySAP Mill Products: A Look Ahead

Further development of the SAP solutions for the metal, paper and textile industries will follow the future use of the Internet, as a technical basis, for the improvement of business processes along the entire logistics chain. It is already clear that core processes from logistics areas such as order processing, production planning and assembly will be oriented even more strongly to the requirements of each industry.

For the next two years, development for the mill products industry will focus on the expansion of retail and distribution scenarios. Development seeks to lower the effort involved in entering mass data that involves a high number of order items in retail with numerous product characteristics. It seeks to accomplish the same task for special processes (plating and cutting processes, for example) that occur in retail or service centres in the metal and paper industry. SAP also works intensively on optimization procedures for planning and supporting production processing in the mill industry. The specifics of the industry occupy centre stage when mapping production types such as sales-order-related production or make-to-stock production in logistics applications. In this context, production types may change according to manufacturing level.

The close collaboration between customers and consulting partners plays a key role in this development. As a long-term goal, SAP seeks to create additional competitive advantages for manufacturers of mill products by including and using new technologies.

8.3 SAP AT KRUPP STAINLESS STEEL

Krupp Stainless Steel Profile GmbH (KEP)

KEP forms part of the steel sector within the ThyssenKrupp group. It belongs to the area of products that includes sections, cold drawn steel, rolled wire rod, and welding products. With about 1,250 employees and two sites (Siegen-Geisweid and Hagen-Wehringhausen in Germany), KEP delivers high grade structural steel, tool steel and steel that is resistant to rust, acid and heat. As a supplier to the motor industry, among others, it fulfils the requirements of QS 9000 and German DIN ISO 9001.

8.3.1 Preconditions

After successful implementation of SAP R/3 application components SD, MM, PP and certain CO functionality in 1997 (Siegen) and in 1998 (Hagen), FI, CO and MM-PUR were migrated from R/2. Modelling of an HR system also began. A parallel task involved the optimization of the business processes for logistics. KEP uses an internally developed shop floor system to monitor individual pieces and control assembly.

8.3.2 Goals for Use of the SCM Tools

Once the complete integration of SAP R/3 offered the basis for seamless cost transparency, the project looked at improving the production logistics. The following goals occupied centre stage:

- Increased data transparency
- Lowered inventory levels (raw materials and processing stock) and committed funds
- Decreased throughput time for orders
- Optimized capacity planning resulting from integration into company planning and rolling three-month planning
- Creation of a tool for handling exceptions

8.3.3 The Decision for Supply Chain Management in mySAP.com

In light of their positive experience with the use of SAP R/3 and help from TKIS (ThyssenKrupp Information Services), an internal company division that runs both the computer centre and IT consulting, it was decided to implement SAP APO. In addition to this, there were other concerns, such as integration with R/3. Prototyping based upon SAP APO 1.1 showed that SAP APO already implemented essential functions. Given the special requirements of the steel industry, direct cooperation with SAP APO seemed appropriate. The conversion of these specific requirements into reality using SAP APO Release 2.0 represents a decisive step forward.

References

Mark A. Brunelli (1999) 'What Buyers Want from Web Sites', in *Purchasing* Magazine, 16 December.

Leif Eriksen (1999) 'Plant Systems for Mills: One Market or Many?', in *The Report on Manufacturing*, AMR Research, January.

Petri Niittymäki (1999) 'The Effect of E-commerce on Finnish Forest Products Marketing', in *Helsinki School of Economics and Business Administration* 8 November.

mySAP Oil & Gas Industry Solution

Dr Holger Kisker
SAP AG

9.1 THE OIL AND GAS INDUSTRY AT THE THRESHOLD OF THE TWENTY-FIRST CENTURY

Opportunities and challenges

Daniel Yergin called the twentieth century the 'oil century' in his book, *The Price*, which appeared in 1991. Oil, often called black gold, has since triggered economic, ecological and military crises. Today, at the threshold of the twenty-first century, crude oil and its derivatives continue to play a key role in the world economy and in our daily lives (Yergin, 1991).

Multi-faceted challenges face the oil industry at the start of the twenty-first century. Nonetheless, four basic trends characterize the challenges, although accurate predictions on the future of the oil industry are almost impossible. The oil industry has often had to deal with the unexpected, and this will continue in the future. But for the oil industry to enjoy continuing success in the new century, it must analyse and master these trends. The trends consist of the following:

- Technical innovation
- Globalization
- Increased competition
- Customer orientation

Technical
innovation

Ever since Edwin L. Drake discovered oil in Titusville, Pennsylvania, in 1859 and triggered the first oil boom in history, the industry has seen continuous technical improvements. However, technical innovations have never before had the dramatic effects on the oil industry seen in the last decade. During that period the increasing performance of computers and the use of information technology in many areas had a huge influence.

At the beginning of the 1990s, the increasingly powerful computers used in seismic studies enabled the crossover from two- to three-dimensional models with real-time visualization and interpretation. Ultimately, they also enabled four-component procedures. The latter combine compression and shear waves to give seismic studies a completely new quality. At the same time, new drilling techniques enabled the discovery of oil at ever greater ocean depths; in the last ten years some 20 per cent of oil and 6 per cent of gas discoveries have occurred more than 2,500 metres below the surface of the ocean. Such technical improvements have compensated for the depletion of new reserves that contained 70 billion BOE (barrel of oil equivalent) in the 1960s. In the 1990s, these reserves were depleted by 20 billion BOE annually. New seismic exploration methods increased the success rate in this period from 1:10 to 1:5.

In the downstream area as well, computer technology has led to innovative and far-reaching improvements. For example, modern information technology has revolutionized the construction and operation of pipelines. Geographical information systems (GIS) help to determine the routes of new oil and gas connections and monitor existing pipeline networks from satellites in space. At the same time, highly-developed, self-driven detectors, called intelligent pigs, crawl through pipelines, find leaks, discover damage and monitor the condition of pipelines on site.

The rapid growth of the Internet has moved the industry even more than these technical innovations. During the 1970s and 1980s, the industry used information technology primarily to improve internal company processes. In the 1990s, however, this changed, as IT focused on cross-company collaboration. The enormous growth of the Internet shifted the focus of this industry sector to global, virtual economic communities that form the marketplace of the future.

For a strongly asset-oriented industry, such as the oil and gas industry, with its oil platforms, pipelines and refineries, a move on to the Internet represents a much larger step than it might for a production company or financial services firm.

The Internet plays a key role in the discovery and development of new markets and business areas. It demands optimization of existing processes and organizational structures, and therefore contributes to lowering overall costs. Although the industry must consider all four trends (technical innovation, globalization, increased competition and customer orientation) equally, it is the Internet that allows it to meet these challenges with a comprehensive and cost-efficient strategy.

Globalization

With the deregulation and privatization of several previously regulated markets (in Russia, Brazil, India and Indonesia, for example) the global crude oil market has opened up as never before. New markets are waiting to be conquered, and new combatants are entering the arena. State-run companies increasingly cross the previous borders of their business activities and are becoming highly-ranked players in the market.

For example, Saudi Aramco, the largest oil company in the world, has entered a downstream alliance with Shell and Texaco in the US. The Russian company Lukoil has also entered the US downstream market, and the Venezuelan firm PDVSA, along with its subsidiary CITGO, occupies a strong position in that market. Outside the US, the largest oil consumer in the world, previously state-run companies also operate. PDVSA, for example, has entered into a downstream alliance with Veba in Germany; Kuwait operates refineries in Europe and has more than 6,000 petrol stations under the brand name of Q8.

While national oil companies have become active globally, investment by Western oil companies into the newly deregulated oil companies has decreased. After the initial euphoria, significantly less money has flowed from international oil companies to the Russian oil industry. New business areas in other markets take a different form. In Indonesia, Pertamina is on the path to privatization, and three of the largest oil companies in China (China National Offshore Oil Corp., CNPC and China Petroleum Corp.) are preparing to launch an initial public offering (IPO).

Although the new markets offer enormous opportunities, they also involve risks, including the instability of political systems. In addition, proven business procedures must be adjusted to local economic, geographical and legal requirements. Many investors have had to learn this lesson the hard way.

Now the Internet offers access to a market that truly deserves the name 'global'. No one knows how large the virtual market really is. Estimates from 1998 indicated that 115 million people had access to the Internet, and that the number was growing by 15 per cent each month. According to Forrester Research, business-to-business transactions on the Internet will reach a volume of $1.3 billion by 2003 (*Industry Week*, 1999). That estimate represents a 30-fold increase on the 1998 volume. The same forecast sees sales to end customers of $3.2 trillion in the same timescale.

Many oil companies and energy providers have already set up Internet-supported information services. For example, LIFT (Licence Information For Trading) enables companies to announce, sell and exchange drilling licences and assets in the North Sea. The Norwegian oil industry has established SOIL (Secure Oil Information Link), an online information source about applications and services for oil companies, service providers and vendors operating on the Norwegian coast.

The Internet is not only the preferred information source, it is also the primary area for future business activities. E-business and e-procurement initiatives have recently begun throughout the oil industry. Cooperative networks allow companies to optimize sales and production while considering the interests of their partners. This approach represents a decisive step towards meeting the challenges of the global market and increased competition.

Increased competition

The profit margins in the oil industry have never been smaller; the need to pare down costs has never been greater than at the present. Oil prices have just recovered from their low point in 1999 and still fluctuate strongly. These realities mean that oil companies must continually adjust their strategies to rapidly-changing market conditions.

Some oil companies have reacted by carrying out mergers, takeovers, alliances, asset exchanges and the sale or outsourcing of activities that do not belong to their core area. It's no coincidence that the largest corporate mergers in history have taken place over the last few years, particularly in the oil industry. Mergers provide companies with access to new technologies, new oil reserves and the capital necessary to remain competitive in the battle for limited resources.

The planned takeover of Arco by BP Amoco, for example, will not lead BP Amoco to a position of supremacy in Alaska. It will secure important oil reserves for the company over the long term. At the same time, structural changes, mergers and takeovers offer the companies involved the opportunity to optimize their organizational structure and to pare down their business processes. Exxon-Mobil and BP-Amoco-Arco, for example, hope that their mergers and restructuring efforts will lead to annual cost savings of $2.8 and $2 billion respectively. Additional mergers will occur, partly for this reason, not only among the large oil companies, but with smaller representatives of the industry as well.

On the one hand, oil companies strengthen their core areas by mergers and takeovers. On the other hand, they increasingly exclude more and more business areas. For example, many companies no longer regard drilling technology and transportation as part of their core business. The outsourcing of IT departments offers yet another example of companies' concentration on their core business. At the beginning of 2000, BP Amoco and Accenture (formerly known as Andersen Consulting) closed the largest outsourcing agreement in the history of downstream business, a deal worth $200 million. In the context of a ten-year contract, Accenture will handle credit card processing, vendor accounting, petrol station settlement, financial analysis and other services in the areas of refineries and marketing for BP Amoco in the US.

The trend toward basing IT systems on best business practices is no longer limited to large companies; it runs through all levels of the market. Unlike twenty years ago, when only large corporate groups could afford specialized IT departments and ERP solutions, today all companies have the opportunity to implement best business practices in the form of preconfigured standard solutions at a good price and in a short time.

The competition for market share will be decided on two sides: efficient operation and sufficient reserves at the drilling site, along with satisfied customers on the sales side.

Customer
orientation

New, open markets demand a stronger orientation toward customers. Customer satisfaction and loyalty must be increased. The competition waits in the supermarket next door or only a click away on the Internet. Customer relationship management is the key. It must find the ideal customers, make contact with them, offer them the products and services they need, and link them to companies with attractive loyalty programmes. The oil industry must undertake the task of turning mass goods into individual solutions.

The petrol station business provides a good example of changing traditional product offerings into individual services. Many oil companies today earn higher revenues by selling soft drinks and confectionery at petrol station convenience shops than they do by selling fuel. The industry is still experimenting with different strategies for business at petrol stations. In Germany, 90 per cent of all petrol stations operate as codos (company owned–dealer operated): the fuel belongs to the oil company, but the dealer owns the station itself.

Shrinking profit margins for fuel sales and increasing profits in convenience products have caused the industry to expand its control over petrol stations. For example, Shell has recently begun to operate its own Select Shops in Germany. In the UK, most petrol stations are cocos (company owned–company operated), while in the US, where some retailers control large distribution networks across the entire country, dodos (dealer owned–dealer operated) play an important role. For survival, the petrol station business must have clear and consistent marketing policies throughout the entire distribution network. Increasing competition requires a strong market name as the most important requirement for customer loyalty in an increasingly global market. The purchase of the ARAL brand by the Veba group is a good example of this trend.

While more and more oil companies open shops at petrol stations, more and more supermarkets are selling fuel. In France, supermarkets with petrol stations already control 40 per cent of the market for fuel products. Similar figures apply to the UK. One option for the oil industry to work against this trend involves alliances and joint ventures with supermarkets. The new Mango Stations in Scandinavia, a joint venture of Statoil and the retail chain ICA/Hakon, is a good example of super petrol stations that provide the size and product offerings of a medium-sized supermarket. The trend is clearly moving to fewer and larger petrol stations with attached shops and fast food restaurants. If the trend continues, the sale of fuel for vehicles will one day become a small incidental business that is integrated into the car parks of large shopping centres.

If oil companies want to retain their existing petrol stations, they must combine the advantages of the locations that they own with individual services. The Internet can provide contact with customers. For example, customers could plan their travel routes along a company's network of petrol stations, and use the Internet to pre-order things they need for the trip; anything from a hot meal during a travel break to a grocery order they can pick up on the way home from the office.

In addition to offering individualized products and services, the environmental awareness of companies also influences customer behaviour. As examples, consider the oil spill after the accident involving the Exxon Valdez on the Alaskan coast, or the case of Brent Spar that cost the Shell group in Germany millions because of adverse customer reaction. In the meantime, most oil companies, and certainly all the large companies, have made tremendous progress in protecting the environment in the context of their business activities. They will surely continue to do so in the future.

The reality that many people consider oil to be one of the worst polluters of the environment and the main cause of global warming has forced oil companies into action. In the final analysis, it doesn't matter if increased burning of fossil fuels really causes the greenhouse effect. What matters is how customers perceive the problem and how oil companies react to it. The successful oil company of the future will have to increase its customer orientation. Individual products and services, attractive loyalty programmes and a friendly image are the decisive factors for successful customer relationship management.

Summary

At the beginning of the twenty-first century, the oil industry sees itself facing numerous challenges. The size of the challenges also offers a huge opportunity: the Internet. The choice of the right information technology and the right Internet strategy will separate the successful from the less successful oil and gas companies in the future. The Internet offers the oil industry the key to mastering the great challenges it faces. It is the most important current technical innovation and the portal to globalization. It is the most efficient tool for heightened competition and it offers the quickest road to customer orientation.

9.2 mySAP OIL & GAS: READY FOR THE CHALLENGES OF THE NEW CENTURY

Overview

With more than 500 customers and over 700 installations worldwide, mySAP Oil & Gas is the leading software solution for the oil and gas industry. mySAP Oil & Gas customers include companies of all sizes, including all those listed in the Fortune Global 100.

The success of the SAP solution began in 1992 with the appearance of R/2 IS-Oil, the first industry solution specifically tailored to the needs of the oil industry. At that time, IS-Oil was based upon the R/2 System for mainframe computers. SAP developed the product in collaboration with Mobil in Europe. To expand the functional scope to include the oil industry's global activities and to use the client/server architecture of SAP R/3, SAP began to develop mySAP Oil & Gas in 1994 – parallel to the development of the first R/3 release.

To guarantee that mySAP Oil & Gas met the industry's requirements to the greatest possible extent, SAP worked in close collaboration with oil companies from the very beginning. The starting group of ten development partners (Chevron, Crown, Elf, Exxon, Mobil, Petrofina, Star, Shell, Sunoco and Texaco) later became the global SAP Oil & Gas Industry Advisory Council, whose members are elected annually by all SAP customers in the oil and gas industry.

In addition to the global Industry Advisory Council, three regional groups are available to interested customers: Europe, the Near East and Africa; the Americas; and the Asia-Pacific rim. Topic-specific focus groups ensure that SAP works closely with industry representatives and will always offer the oil and gas industry the best possible solution in the future.

9.2.1 mySAP Oil & Gas – The Complete Solution for the Oil and Gas Industry

The SAP Oil & Gas Solution Map

mySAP Oil & Gas covers the entire value-added chain in the oil and gas industry, from the drilling site to the gas pump. The mySAP Oil & Gas Solution Map (*see* Table 9.1), developed in collaboration with representatives of the industry, describes the processes involved. It is the central tool for communication between SAP and its customers in the oil and gas industry: from first contact to system implementation and to a long-term partnership. It aims at ensuring that customers derive the maximum possible benefit from their investment. Oil companies also use the Solution Map to process their own internal projects.

Exploration & production

mySAP Oil & Gas contains a complete solution in the upstream area for joint-venture accounting and production sharing. It enables the sharing of costs between joint-venture partners and adherence to governmental restrictions for production sharing. The E&P (Exploration and Production) module contains functions for maintaining complex production networks, calculating conveyance quantities, processing revenue accounting and gas asset accounting among the participating partners. E&P links geotechnical data from external systems with conveyance and accounting; it integrates production processes with maintenance processes of above and underground assets (maintenance, repair and overhaul (MRO)).

mySAP Supply Chain Management for the oil and gas industry

mySAP Oil & Gas handles the entire spectrum of hydrocarbon products: gas, LNG, gasoline and bitumen. When necessary, it considers density, temperature, pressure and calorific value. The system monitors consignment and mixed stock in storage tanks and tracks in-transit stocks for all types of transport (ship, railway, lorry and pipeline) from loading through to delivery. Freight costs, profits and losses from waste are calculated section-by-section according to the FIFO principle. Open interfaces to terminal automation systems (TAS) and solutions for transportation optimization (transport planning interface, TPI) provide a seamless integration of external productions in mySAP Oil & Gas.

The Trader's & Scheduler's Workbench (TSW) contributes to maintaining an efficient balance between supply and demand in the supply chain. It monitors current and future stocks at various locations and transportation systems. It also integrates market information, planned and nominated goods movements, production data, consumption predictions and replenishment forecasts. Simulation functions, an alert monitor for exception handling and an open interface for the exchange of transportation nominations and confirmations between oil companies and transportation partners (such as pipeline operators) round out the functions for efficient processing of the complete supply chain for hydrocarbon products.

Downstream marketing

The solution for the downstream area of mySAP Oil & Gas covers commercial exploitation, from price determination based upon current exchange data to contract management, and from order execution to petrol station sales. The form-based price-determination functions can calculate interim, final and differential prices based upon current market data and the exchange rates of external service providers. A comprehensive solution administers the company's swap business with its swap partners, monitors

TABLE 9.1   Oil & Gas Solution Map

Enterprise Management	Strategic Enterprise Management	Business Intelligence	Managerial Accounting	Financial Accounting	Regulatory Compliance	Joint Venture Management
Customer Relationship Management	Customer Service	Product/Brand Marketing	Marketing Programme Management	Sales Management	Service Agreements	Service Fulfilment
Exploration & Production	Exploration & Appraisal	Development	Production	Marketing	Disposal	
Supply	Supply Chain Optimization & Planning	Acquire, Trade & Sell	Exchange & Throughput Handling	Scheduling	Inventory Management	Primary Distribution & Transport
Manufacturing	Manufacturing Planning & Optimization	Process Management	Gas & Fuel Manufacturing	Lubes Manufacturing	Blending & Packaging	Product Quality Management
Market	Marketing	Contracts & Pricing	Commercial Sales	Secondary Distribution & Transportation		
Service Station & Convenience Retailing	Category Management	Transaction Processing & Settlement	Retail Network Management	Inventory Management	Site Management	
Business Support	Human Resource Core Functions & Strategy	Human Resource Analytics & Enabling Solutions	Procurement	Treasury/Corporate Finance Management	Fixed Asset Management	Engineering, Construction & Maintenance

the corresponding goods movements of both partners, and enables online (Internet) reconciliation of all these goods movements and financial transactions with the partner.

In addition, mySAP Oil & Gas contains a Service Station Retail (SSR) component, a complete solution for efficient processing of petrol station business. SSR handles wet business as well as the increasingly important dry business of shops at petrol stations. This feature includes an attractive range of goods, efficient replenishment planning, successful advertising campaigns and flexible pricing based upon analysis of the local competition – crucial survival functions in today's petrol station business.

mySAP Oil & Gas is currently the most comprehensive solution for the oil and gas industry. The product fulfils all the requirements of the value-added chain typical to the industry and can therefore successfully handle all the challenges that tomorrow will bring.

9.2.2 mySAP Oil & Gas – Answers to the Challenges of the Twenty-First Century

mySAP Oil & Gas is well prepared for technological innovation, globalization, increased competition and customer orientation. The software uses the most modern technical innovations for electronic commerce on the Internet. In combination with mySAP.com, the global e-business platform, mySAP Oil & Gas becomes an open and cooperative business environment for personalized and requirement-based solutions.

Efficient software solutions that use proven business procedures have always offered a strategic way to increase competitiveness and to reduce costs. Since its initial appearance, mySAP Oil & Gas has helped the competitiveness of oil companies by optimizing business processes and ending cost-intensive legacy systems. Mobil US is a good example of the latter. In 1999, the group replaced more than 300 legacy systems with mySAP Oil & Gas. The legacy systems operated in the upstream, downstream and financial areas; many were not Y2K compliant.

The uniformity of IT platforms also contributes to cost reductions in companies that react to increased competition with mergers. BP Amoco, Exxon-Mobil and Total-Fina all used mySAP Oil & Gas before their mergers, and mySAP Oil & Gas will help them to achieve the goals of their mergers.

9.3   EXAMPLES OF SUCCESSFUL IMPLEMENTATION OF MySAP OIL & GAS

This section introduces two examples of successful implementation of mySAP Oil & Gas in the oil industry, one from the upstream area and one from the downstream area. Further information on the implementations and Chevron USA Production and Shell Austria, along with other sample implementations, can be found at the mySAP Oil & Gas Media Center: www.sap.com/oilgas.

9.3.1 Chevron USA Production

The Chevron USA Production Company is the exploration and production branch of the Chevron Corporation. It has around 4,500 employees and produces 343,000 barrels (bbl) of oil and 55,000 m³ of gas each day. Chevron USA is involved in 3,500 joint ventures and bills its 1,400 partners some $50 million each month. Prior to the implementation of mySAP Oil & Gas the company used 200 individual financial applications. This approach led to excessive costs, insufficient data integrity and a lack of up-to-date information. Rob Plath, leader of SAP support at Chevron, said:

> mySAP Oil & Gas is linked with standard applications in SAP R/3 to create all the data we need for our joint ventures. We use the industry-specific functions of mySAP Oil & Gas to calculate specific items such as cash receivables, common cost surcharges and the partner portion of common cost surcharges and to generate invoices for our partners. mySAP Oil & Gas has significantly increased the integrity of data when comparing our monthly costs with those of our partners . . . through the use of one integrated system we could not only increase the efficiency of our processes, but also improve relationships with our partners. Now we can react more quickly and more specifically to questions about our monthly invoicing procedures.

In addition to functions for financials, controlling and joint-venture billing, Chevron USA uses the following SAP R/3 application components: Materials Management, Plant Maintenance and Project System. According to Plath:

> The R/3 Project System processes all the work involved in a project in the context of our joint ventures. Some of our cooperative activities require the approval of our partners for large undertakings, such as drilling a new well or overhauling a drilling platform. As soon as we have the approval, we set up the project, execute it, and create monthly reports on project activities for our partners. The R/3 Project System supports us in all these activities.

Large portions of the overall project were first implemented at a Chevron subsidiary, Warren Petroleum. Project teams consisting primarily of Chevron employees then used a standard procedure for the design, structure and implementation and rolled out the project in other areas. At the centre stood the creation of common business processes; the definition of tasks, roles and responsibilities; the design of work templates; and the implementation of team functions. The team functions included starter kits that enabled new team members to quickly become familiar with their roles. Chevron emphasized standard training measures along with consistent, reusable interfaces to minimize the effort involved in additional implementations.

Chevron is a member of the global SAP Oil & Gas Industry Advisory Council, and Rob Plath serves as Chair of the SAP Oil & Gas Upstream Focus Group.

We find ourselves in an outstanding partnership with SAP regarding the development of mySAP Oil & Gas. We work closely with SAP project managers and development managers. Along with them, we determine options for improving and enhancing the functions of mySAP Oil & Gas.

In the meantime, Chevron has significantly expanded the use of mySAP Oil & Gas and started to implement the solution for its downstream business as well. In addition to the Human Resources application component, Chevron will use the SAP Trader's & Scheduler's Workbench and the SAP Business Information Warehouse along with its industry-specific enhancements in its lubricant, asphalt and fuel businesses.

9.3.2 Shell Austria

For Shell Austria, a subsidiary of Royal Dutch/Shell, the implementation of mySAP Oil & Gas acted as a pilot project for the worldwide Shell Group. Shell Austria concentrates on the sale of oil products. Inadequate functions for these and other business activities, a lack of transparency and the need to reduce operating costs moved Shell Austria to replace its legacy system. The company uses mySAP Oil & Gas for deliveries to petrol stations, airports, industrial customers and for processing swap business.

The installation includes the following components: Financials, Asset Management, Controlling, Sales and Distribution, Materials Management, Investment Management, Human Resources and the entire spectrum of industry-specific, downstream functions. As one of the original ten industry partners and a current member of the SAP Oil & Gas Industry Advisory Council, Shell plays an active role in the development of mySAP Oil & Gas. It shares its knowledge with SAP developers, particularly regarding the management of hydrocarbons, the transportation and distribution of fuels and oil tax processing. Shell Services International (SSI) works with SAP to create an industry template for mySAP Oil & Gas, a part of the Best Business Practices for the oil and gas industry that contributes to quick and efficient system implementation. Shell transferred its company-specific template to mySAP Oil & Gas during development of the prototype and during detailed development of the system to further accelerate and simplify the implementation process.

Shell Austria saw the advantages of the change to mySAP Oil & Gas a few months before the start of productive operations. The level of integration in SAP Oil & Gas enabled significantly better data flow and made the company more transparent. It could monitor the logistics and value-added chain more easily and meet customer requirements more quickly. Shell Austria has now partially automated procurement, which enables the optimization of purchasing, a reduction in costs and, most importantly, clear purchasing and processing policies.

More consistent and precise data has improved requirements estimates and increased the reliability of suppliers. The introduction of a transfer pricing system has helped to optimize business processes between two business units, sales and distribution and logistics. Customer service has also benefited from precise information, especially regarding delivery times for lubricants. Efficient supply management has improved deliveries to petrol stations.

Shell Austria has performed pioneering work in the Royal Dutch/Shell Group. Additional subsidiaries and sectors of the Group in Europe (Germany, France and the UK), Asia (Singapore and Japan), South America (Venezuela and Brazil) and Australia now work successfully with mySAP Oil & Gas.

References

Daniel Yergin (1991) *The Prize: The Epic Quest for Oil, Money, and Power*, New York: Simon & Schuster.

Industry Week, 'Net Gains – E-Commerce Is Poised to Follow', 17 May 1999.

mySAP Financials – Real Estate

Volker Zimmermann, SAP AG, Helen Apps, SAP AG
and Kay Smagowicz, SAP AG

10.1 URGENT NEED FOR PROFESSIONAL MANAGEMENT

In the past, drives to increase efficiency have, for the most part, been concentrated on production and human resources. Improvements to production and personnel management methods have commanded centre stage. The arrival of the global network and Internet technology has lent whole new dimensions to supply chain management and e-commerce. Maximizing the business benefits to be gained from the management of real estate has stubbornly remained (and to some extent still remains) a secondary consideration despite the fact that:

- 30 per cent of the national wealth is in real estate
- The rental management of one square metre of usable floor area costs up to $30 per month
- Real estate comprises 30 per cent of your balance sheet total

In a business environment characterized by fierce competition and rapid change, the need for professional real estate management is becoming increasingly urgent. Whether your customers are commercial or residential tenants or internal departments, you need to respond quickly and efficiently to your customers' needs, reduce operational cost while increasing the value of your real estate portfolio.

mySAP Financials Real Estate enables you to become more customer and market focused and more flexible in your response to changing circumstances and the demands of both your customers and the market.

You want to offer your customers a more efficient and flexible service, reduce operational costs and increase the value of your portfolio.

What you need is a comprehensive software solution, which encompasses the following functionalities:

- Seamless integration of your real estate management software with your company's software. Integration, which is especially crucial in the areas of maintenance planning and processing, financial accounting, controlling and project development

- Transparency of costs and revenues according to a wide variety of criteria

- Portfolio analysis and simulation possibilities

- Flexible tools for day-to-day management of your real estate properties

- Internet-enabled front-end offices for tenant information and application processing

mySAP Financials Real Estate has two target groups:

- Corporates, i.e. companies that do not trade real estate, but have recognized the importance of efficient controlling and management of their own or leased-in real estate

- Investors, i.e. companies that trade real estate, be it as a project developer, provider of office and commercial space, facility or property manager or as a residential rental concern

Today mySAP Financials Real Estate offers you:

- A unique software solution for Real Estate Management that is fully integrated with one of the market leaders in business software systems

- A unique software solution for Real Estate Management that – thanks to its wide range of functions – is the perfect solution for managing your portfolio, be it for corporate or investment purposes

- A unique software solution for Real Estate Management with an interface to the Internet: mySAP Workplace, mySAP Marketplace and mySAP.com collaborative business scenarios. These solutions bring together your employees, customers, business partners, interested parties and all the aspects of your business so that all the information you could ever want is on the web and, literally, at your fingertips

mySAP FINANCIALS REAL ESTATE VALUE PROPOSITION

10.2.1 Seamless Integration with the World's leading Financial Software

Functional areas of mySAP Financials include the following:

Financial Operations – Enables collaboration among enterprises and within their business network using defined business policies and shared services to handle all customer and supply-chain-related financial processes. It helps to automate the financial supply chain using web and new electronic service models.

Accounting – Records quantities and values from financially relevant transactions out of value-creating processes and maintains a consistent, reconciled, auditable set of books for statutory reporting and management support. It also serves as a reliable source for analytic applications.

Strategy & Enterprise Management – Enables companies to execute strategies fast and successfully and manage business performance throughout the entire organization. It supports integrated strategic planning, performance monitoring, business consolidation and effective stakeholder communication thus enabling value-based management.

10.2.2 Business Analytics

Business Analytics in general and Real Estate Business Analytics in particular are based on SAP's Strategic Enterprise Management (SAP SEM). SAP SEM is a set of software functions and processes that enables executives and senior managers to implement and operate management processes across the organization. SAP SEM helps executives to simulate, analyze, monitor, optimize and communicate the strategic aspects of the enterprise. It supports profit-oriented strategies to improve overall corporate value.

SAP SEM incorporates the perspective of stakeholders who share in the long-term success of the company. These stakeholders include employees, investors, customers and local and regional governments. With SAP SEM, corporations are able, for example, based on the Balanced Scorecard concept, to translate strategy into action faster and enable knowledge sharing and learning throughout the entire organization to continue improving strategy and optimizing its execution.

In essence, this means that you can compare the information you have on your Real Estate objects with market information by using information extracted from R/3 by the SAP Business Information Warehouse (BW) and comparing it with information from local markets published on the Internet. At a glance, you can see how your objects compare to others on the market. And you can view it all in the convenient MS-Excel front end of SAP BW.

You map your portfolio according to any criteria (location, size, usage, revenue,

TABLE 10.1 Real Estate Solution Map

Financials	Strategy & Enterprise Management	Accounting	Financial Operations			
Real Estate Business Analytics	Valuation Methods	Scoring Model Time scale	Benchmarking & Reporting	Planning & Simulation	Data Exchange and Interfaces	Exit Strategies
E-business	Real Estate Marketplace	B2C Processes	B2B Processes	Customer Relationship Management	Marketing Programme Management	
Project Management	General Legal Frameword	Approximate Financial Planning & Time Scale	Bid Invitation, Award, Invoicing	Ready for Use		
Commercial Management	Contract Management	Rental Accounting	Adjustment & Sales-Based Rent	Service Charge Settlement	Land Use Management	Third Party Management
Technical & Infrastructure Management	Space Management	Planned Maintenance	Repairs & Modernization	Procurement of External Services	Energy Management	Building Control Systems
Real Estate Controlling	Object Controlling	Responsibility Accounting with Profit Centres	Overhead Cost Controlling	Activity-Based Costing		
System & Real Estate Infrastructure	ITS Workplace	Organizational Structure	Master Date Objects	Partner & Address Management	Correspondence & Optical Archive	Graphical Interface	Reporting

costs and so on. In future releases, SAP will also offer simulation options with parameters such as indexing, interest increases, inflation, over/under rented, duration of contracts, location evaluation of the objects, and so on. Business alternatives such as make or buy, sale and lease-back are also included in these parameters.

These functions provide you with a full-blown real estate portfolio management system including several methods (e.g. DCF or investment method) to determine the market value of real estate assets. Furthermore, KPIs, simulation scenarios and what-if analysis support you in making strategic decisions. The results can be seen in detail reports, overview lists or visualized via portfolio graphics. These tools enable you to analyze business alternatives such as buy, sale or lease-back.

10.2.3 E-Business

10.2.3.1 Market Places – Portals – B2B – B2C

The pulse of your marketing and sales activities is the sky7 portal, an e-commerce solution tailor-made for the real estate industry. By setting up your own real estate portal, you can automatically display future vacancies on the Internet. It is designed to help real estate portals live up to the demands and expectations of each user by means of individually adaptable configurations and optimum functionality. Based on the mySAP.com solution portfolio, sky7 not only fulfils the technological requirements of a real estate portal, it also integrates both editorial content and a network for providing additional services.

Selected objects can be automatically transferred between your mySAP Financials Real Estate system and your Internet portal on a regular basis (and back to your prospect administration system). The search engine supports object searches according to a wide range of criteria such as rent, fixtures and fittings, size of space, etc. A geographical information system is also available for the search and for mapping infrastructure data such as transport connections and local points of interest. Your sky7 real estate portal can be accessed by anybody interested in locating rental objects. Favourite lists can be created and concluding contracts is a much easier process as you already have all the important data in the system.

In the e-business segment Business-to-Consumer (B2C), portals offer a web-based communication platform for real estate companies with tenants, owners of real estate and their employees as well as with service partners. These platforms are integrated in the existing business processes and are available to users round the clock. Portals sink the process costs and improve the general cost transparency, while increasing customer retention and partner satisfaction.

Business-to-Business (B2B) focuses on the optimization of communication between all parties involved in real estate management (owner, investor, property manager, tenant and maintenance teams, etc.) and provides process optimization between organizations over the Internet. B2B provides a forum for simplifying construction projections and the exchange of related documentation. B2B Procurement provides real estate organizations with the means to optimize their procurement processes for goods and services. The bid invitation procedure is standardized and distributed to a much wider public. The vendor selection process and the awarding of contracts is vastly simplified and automated.

10.2.3.2 Customer Relationship Management

The SAP Customer Interaction Center provides you with a hub, whether it be physical or virtual, that conducts the tele-business of your organization. Tele-business can be comprised of any or all the following: Tele-Sales (inbound and outbound), Tele-Marketing (inbound and outbound) or Tele-Service (inbound). Call Center representatives use aids such as telephony tools (Computer Telephony Interface – CTI), scripts, predictive dialing mechanisms, etc. The call centre can act as a revenue generator, a centre for lead generation, a fulfilment house, a repair centre, a service dispatch hub or executor of any other business practice that can be facilitated via the telephone. Call Centers are evolving into Contact Centers or Customer Interaction Centers. Help desks and technical support organizations are usually separate and distinct organizations from the traditional call centre.

10.2.4 Project Development

As a project developer, you need information about the legal aspects of usage, attested usage rights for third parties, contamination, transfer of uses and encumbrances, usufructuary rights, and other easements and rights at your fingertips during the planning phase. Use the SAP Document Management together with the project or definition of the property to store this information electronically. Use the Land Use Management Information System (currently under development) to manage the land register data, and to map the public authority view on rights and obligations, encumbrances and restrictions.

Use the general Real Estate contract to store contract information such as purchase price, documents, participating partners, deadlines and so on. You can also use the general Real Estate contract to map rental premises. In the same way, you can store provisional contracts with maintenance teams to ensure that the legal requirements of the project are covered, store declarations of assignments in the planning phase using this contract tool or SAP Document Management.

Once the project has been launched, use the SAP Project System (PS) to divide the project according to maintenance groups or service specifications, to structure the project flow using the networked processes and for allocating the necessary resources (materials, personnel, services) from the breakdown plans. You can collect the requirements and specifications in the breakdown plans and map any restrictions for quantities, delivery content, quality, scheduling and offer validity. mySAP.com Collaborative Projects offers you comprehensive support for allocating part tasks or maintenance teams to external service providers. On the Internet, you can place the bid invitation, view offers, view reports on the project process even during the project execution, make any necessary changes to plans and documents and complete any other tasks required for the smooth running of the project. The usual amount of time wasted due to .wrongly addressed faxes, business trips and meetings is drastically reduced.

10.2.5 Commercial Management

10.2.5.1 Management of Interested Parties

The Management of Interested Parties in mySAP Financials Real Estate collects requests that have been submitted on the Internet or by traditional methods such as post, telephone or fax. If there are any special entitlements to occupancy for a certain space/residential unit then you enter them directly in the object. You can store the rental requests in the system and periodically compare them with your portfolio or vacant spaces/rental units. If there is a match, you can create a contract offer and send it to the interested party.

10.2.5.2 Contract Management

mySAP Financials Real Estate Contract Management allows you to map various contract terms, conditions and options, as well as partner information. The link to the general ledger is derived from the conditions. The direct integration to SAP Document Management enables you to store all paperwork in electronic format with the system objects.

A period program that usually runs monthly automatically posts the due items in the general ledger and creates open items for the accounts payable or accounts receivable.

10.2.5.3 Rental Accounting

The rental accounting is closely integrated with mySAP Financials Accounting. A vendor contract partner is created for the lease-in contracts and a customer contract partner is created for the lease-out contracts. The periodic posting runs for the subledger accounts generate open items. You can set the cost and revenue accounts for posting for each condition type, for example, for posting the rent to other accounts as service charges. mySAP Financials Accounting also supports you with dunning functions and dunning charges. Interest on arrears can be calculated as required. A full correspondence function supports these transactions.

10.2.5.4 Rent Adjustment

As a tenant, you need information about any future rent adjustments for planning purposes to ensure that your payments are adjusted accordingly. As a landlord, this information is one of the key factors for the commercial success of your venture. They must be conducted in a timely matter and within the given legal framework. mySAP Financials Real Estate supports a huge variety of rent adjustment methods. A periodic program detects all rental units where an adjustment could be made and automatically proposes the best possible adjustment. The system supports all related correspondence to affected tenants prior to activating the adjustment to get their approval.

10.2.5.5 Sales-Based Rent

The system offers you comprehensive support for sales-based (turnover) rents that are particularly prevalent in areas of retail real estate (shopping centres, airports, stations and stores). These contracts enable you to define the sales-based rent as a percentage rate of the target sales, as a graduated rent or a fixed amount. Alternatively, you can use quantities as reference factors for products sold instead of the target sales figures. An interface is available for transferring sales reports to your R/3 System from outside sources. For example, via Internet access responsible personnel can enter the sales data directly.

10.2.5.6 Service Charge Settlement

In many properties, the service charges have already become the second rent. An integral part of professional real estate management is offering or purchasing a wide range of services at competitive prices. It is especially important for the service charge settlements to be created on time and passed on to the tenant. You use the purchasing functions in SAP to map the utility services. You can group your Real Estate objects accordingly in settlement units and assign the purchase order of all utilities and other services to these settlement units. When the goods or services are delivered, you can reference them to your purchase order. The system automatically creates the corresponding payable vendor invoice. You can pass on the service charges to the tenant by using an agreed flat rate without a detailed service charge settlement. In addition, SAP also supports you with periodic advance payment function, which can be then settled for a user-specified period.

10.2.5.7 Third-Party Management

Outsourcing is an ever-growing trend in real estate. In the role of third-party manager, you are responsible for managing real estate, from locating potential tenants to rent collection through to services such as service charge settlement, surplus-revenue invoices, plant maintenance, room and space management and so on. The above sections have already given you a taste of what mySAP Marketplace for Real Estate objects can offer you. There is a special management contract for mapping the fees that are due to you for your management services. In this contract, you specify the services you will provide and the fees the landlord of the property will be charged. These fees can depend either on the sales (rent revenues) or be event dependent. Management fees are posted simultaneously on the vendor side in your company accounts and on the customer side in the accounts of the object being managed.

10.2.6 Technical and Infrastructure Management

10.2.6.1 Space Management

Spaces or rooms are available as special master data objects in mySAP Financials Real Estate for your professional room and space management. You can integrate CAD and CAFM graphical systems with these objects using a standard SAP interface. These objects can then be directly maintained in the graphical systems and the updated data transferred to the SAP system. SAP works together with a considerable number of leading graphics providers. More subjects that are currently under development include:

- Relocation planning – relocation plans that are created in the graphical system are transferred to mySAP Financials Real Estate. The condition of the rooms and spaces are automatically changed. If required, the necessary service personnel can be scheduled, assigned and invoiced using SAP PM functions
- Integrated materials requirements planning – in the long term, we want to integrate the planning of personnel, IT and space requirements. In connection with this, the linking of rooms and spaces to equipment from SAP PM and personnel master data in SAP Human Resources (HR) is planned

10.2.6.2 Maintenance and Inspection

Property maintenance and inspection are the classical parts of Facilities Management. In mySAP Financials Real Estate, you can link all the relevant Real Estate objects with functional locations from SAP Plant Maintenance (PM). All related functions available in PM can be used for Real Estate objects. Any due costs can be displayed together with other real estate costs in integrated reporting.

You can use maintenance plans to map scheduled maintenance for your objects in the system. These plans can be based on previous bills of material or work plan and structured maintenance tasks networks or hierarchies.

When a maintenance needs to take place, the system displays a description of the maintenance and inspection tasks that are to be carried out. The schedule dates of your maintenance plan provide an invaluable alarm function for deadlines. This ensures that important inspections such as fire safety checks are not missed. In cases when the maintenance is done internally, the Automatic Scheduler and the Resource Scheduler insure that the right person is scheduled to the specific task.

Once the task is concluded, following tasks and reports can be distributed either manually or by mobile devices such as Palm Pilots or WAP mobiles.

In cases when you need to use services of external providers, SAP Materials Management (MM) supports you in the related decision process. Bundling of maintenance orders in accordance with various criteria such as preferred service providers lets you award your orders to the external company that offers you the best conditions. mySAP Financials Real Estate herewith offers you the most important prerequisites needed to drastically reduce costs in Facilities Management defining standards that are compulsory for the whole company:

■ Procurement strategy

■ Service catalogues and service specifications

■ Required services and corresponding service levels

■ Preferred or sole materials to be used for Real Estate objects or usage types

10.2.6.3 Repairs

In addition to the functions for executing planned maintenance, unplanned repair can also be easily tracked in the system. The integration of SAP Plant Maintenance (SAP PM) and mySAP Financials Real Estate enables you to set up a hierarchy of maintenance objects or areas that can correspond to the hierarchy of the property you are managing. Due to this configuration you can create malfunction reports with direct reference to your Real Estate objects. Such malfunctions can also be entered directly via the Internet and mobile telephones. If a malfunction report is considered valid a maintenance order is created. This order offers you comprehensive support in completing the specific repair. The costs of both planned and unplanned maintenance are collected in maintenance orders. These orders can be displayed in your Real Estate hierarchy in relevant cost and revenue reports.

10.2.7 Real Estate Controlling

Every Real Estate object in mySAP Financials Real Estate is also an object in SAP Controlling (CO object). This direct integration with SAP Controlling gives you access to proven planning functions for cost and activity types as well as to revenues for the Real Estate objects. These include:

■ Cost planning on cost-type level

■ Revenue planning on revenue-type level

■ Cost and revenue planning on period level

■ Planning of direct internal activity allocation where the rates for internal activities are mathematically determined from the internal exchange of activities between cost centres

■ MS-Excel support for online and off-line planning with direct transfer to SAP

In this way you can enter planned costs and revenues on the relevant objects on which the actual value from, for example, rent revenue or maintenance costs, will later accumulate. You can also plan revenue and costs on the level of the building due to the hierarchical structure of the object, while the plan value later accumulates on the rental units. In reporting you can compare the plan values for the building with the actual values of the rental units assigned to the building. This makes the time-consuming and expensive formation of formal structures (such as cost centre hierarchies) redundant. Assigning costs directly to the objects also allows you to view the cost and revenue evaluation from the view of the Real Estate object.

You can enjoy the benefit of SAP Profit Center Accounting to map your results independently of the object structure and the structure of your external financial reporting. Profit centres contain planning functions like those for cost centres. The advantage for you is that you can structure the profit centres as you like and use alternative hierarchies to map, say, the regional view, the usage view and the organizational view.

10.3   CUSTOMER SUCCESS

10.3.1 Frankfurt Airport

With more than 1,000 take-offs and landings daily and an annual freight volume of approximately 1.4 million tons while serving as the home airport and main centre of activity for Lufthansa, the Rhein-Main airport in Frankfurt is not only the largest airport in Germany but also an important key player in the aviation sector, both in Europe and on a global scale.

Frankfurt/Main AG airport is not only responsible for making sure that air traffic services run smoothly, it is also committed to effective real estate management. Frankfurt airport's real estate management focuses on renting out commercial units in the airport terminal, providing service counters for the commercial airlines and managing its own rental business.

Unique to the real estate management industry, Frankfurt airport looks after an airport complex whose real estate portfolio, although limited to one location just outside of Frankfurt, is nevertheless comparable to other commercial portfolios in its complexity and diversity. Frankfurt airport currently manages approximately 400 buildings of various size and use ranging from airline terminals for passenger services to office buildings and repair hangars used to service major airlines. Many objects are assigned additional properties that serve a special function, such as freight and luggage logistics or airplane ground servicing. The individual rental units, numbering more than 25,000, are rented to both internal and external tenants.

Frankfurt airport recognized the need for an integrated software solution at a very early stage. Various factors contributed to the decision to introduce mySAP Financials Real Estate for its real estate management, such as the need for reliable audits, a high-performance real estate controlling program and a consolidated dataset. In addition to those requirements, the project goal was to implement a system for real estate management that maps all the key processes of the airport's real estate activities. The most important of these are master data management, applicant management, rental and tenant services, rental accounting and invoicing and rent adjustments. The processes defined for each of these activities correspond to the functions provided by mySAP Financials Real Estate, thereby making modifications to the standard system unnecessary. Frankfurt airport's invoicing and reporting functions are two areas that have been improved significantly by the implementation of SAP R/3. An attachment to the lease-out replaces the monthly rent invoices, and is printed automatically using a special reporting program only when fundamental changes are made to the lease-out, for example condition adjustments. This has allowed the airport to realize considerable savings by reducing the amount of paper used in the daily routine. With the introduction of a real-time online reporting program, paper printouts and their distribution are no longer necessary, and the profitability and general overview of the real estate portfolio become much more transparent. Acceptance of the system by Frankfurt airport employees has been heightened by the online availability of detailed information for all users, the elimination of manual distribution tasks and the increased level of responsibility for each user.

One very significant aspect of the implementation of mySAP Financials Real Estate was the need to uphold the productive R/2 System while implementing RE at the same time. Important R/2 functions such as customer management and dunning were also to be used by Real Estate Management, therefore the existing R/2 System had to be linked to the FI, CO and RE components of R/3. This challenge was solved in a short space of time by designing special interface programs for exchanging master data and flow data between the systems, proving the possibility of easy integration between mySAP Financials Real Estate and existing non-SAP accounting systems.

In order to achieve the most effective implementation of the new system, Frankfurt airport had already commissioned Pricewaterhouse Coopers Management Consulting Services (PwC) to perform a feasibility analysis. PwC was also instrumental in the implementation of the new system, drawing on its past experience with a number of successful RE implementations, including the implementation of mySAP Financials Real Estate at Copenhagen airport. Following the design and creation of a prototype system, Frankfurt airport went live as scheduled in August 1999. New hardware also contributed to the success of the project, enabling the posting of approximately 12,000 lease-outs per hour. In the next project phase, the current functions will be enhanced to map the airport's franchise and sales-based lease-outs using RE.

10.3.2 MIB AG Property & Facility Management

MIB AG Property & Facility Management offers property and facilities management services to a variety of leading Swiss companies, such as the Credit Suisse Group. With the support of SAP and outsourcing partner AC Automation Center AG, MIB AG has established a robust and future-proof IT environment capable of supporting its ambitious plans for expansion and internationalization.

Increasingly companies are selectively outsourcing business processes such as payroll and pensions administration, real estate management, supply-chain management or accounting services in order to concentrate on their core competencies. With the right skills, the right IT environment and the right business partners, the corresponding service providers can look forward to rapid and substantial growth. For the best results, three partners must join forces.

- First, the service provider, with his extensive process-specific expertise
- Second, a company that supplies a software solution geared to the specific requirements of the business process to be outsourced
- Third, a partner capable of operating and supporting that solution

In other words, the business process outsourcing provider needs to find the right IT outsourcing partner.

A prime example of a company capable of delivering high-quality, selective outsourcing services is MIB AG. Founded in 1994, this Swiss-based enterprise provides property and facilities management to distinguished names such as ABB, Compaq and Winterthur Insurance. The services of MIB AG™ include the full range of financial and administrative tasks relating to real estate ownership and leasing, repairs and maintenance, facilities management, conversions, sale preparation and investment planning. With 410 employees, MIB AG currently manages over 1,000 commercial properties with a total area of 27 million square feet.

MIB AG wanted to implement a new IT solution capable of supporting its complex and fast growing business. In part this decision was prompted by winning a major new contract from a global player, the Credit Suisse Group, and in part by the inflexibility and high maintenance requirements of its legacy system. MIB AG required a high-performance, cost-effective solution that could keep pace with its fast-expanding customer base – in other words, standard yet powerful software from a reliable partner and deployed on a robust, fully integrated architecture. MIB AG also wanted to outsource its IT infrastructure and the day-to-day operation of that infrastructure, allowing it to concentrate on what it does best: managing real estate. It chose the outsourcing services provider AC Automation Center AG to create a suitable IT client/server infrastructure running SAP R/3 standard software and industry-specific applications. SAP played a supporting role, offering training and onsite assistance to both AC and MIB AG. SAP has recognized the growing importance of business process outsourcing and is eager to partner with companies that provide corresponding services.

MIB chose SAP software for several reasons. R/3 provides a truly integrated and proven platform for a variety of business processes. As standard software, R/3 is ideal for communications and data interchange with partners and customers, but is readily adaptable to individual requirements. It also provides support for multiple languages and multiple currencies (including the euro): all key considerations when serving international customers such as the Credit Suisse Group. Moreover, the RE module offered additional functionality tailored to the needs of real estate management.

The IT environment provided for MIB AG by AC Automation Center AG is based on a client/server architecture, with Compaq ProLiant servers under Windows NT, and an Oracle database. The infrastructure includes WAN connectivity for 10 locations throughout Switzerland, a data centre with backup computers, improved and enhanced local area network functionality and e-mail services. AC manages the central SAP R/3 servers and operates a hotline for all IT-related queries. SAP played a significant role in the project, assisting AC with its own business process experts, providing training for the staff of AC™ as well as project-related support. From the initial contact to the start of operations with the R/3 functions Financial Accounting, Controlling, Asset Accounting and Real Estate, the project took a mere five and a half months. The solution went live on 1 January 1998, initially with 25 users. MIB AG has since implemented Service Management and Plant Maintenance modules and the number of users has soared to 150.

The new outsourced IT infrastructure has benefited MIB AG in a number of ways. It no longer has to contend with a heterogeneous IT landscape, data duplication, maintenance-intensive in-house software developments and the many interfaces between systems. The solution streamlines business processes by providing a single, highly integrated platform, which can be extended and adapted to changing needs and specific customer requirements. On the basis of SAP R/3 and the tailored functionality of the Real Estate module, MIB AG is able to manage its highly complex services with efficiency, and provide its clients with the responsiveness, effectiveness and cost transparency they demand. Moreover, now that it has outsourced the entire infrastructure to AC, MIB AG can concentrate its own resources on its core business: the management of real estate. The combined efforts of AC and SAP ensured that the outsourcing services of MIB™ are now supported by best-in-class solutions right along the line.

Hans Dietz, CEO, MIB AG summarizes: 'As a leading business process outsourcing provider, we want a complete solution, backed by reliable partners, enabling us to set new standards. That is what AC and SAP deliver.'

CHAPTER 11

mySAP Retail Industry Solution

Peter Wesche, SAP AG

11.1 A CHANGING INDUSTRY

Markets

Retail, the second oldest profession in the world, has shown many faces over time. Since the beginning of the twentieth century, economists have attempted to find a systematic explanation for the behaviour of retail commerce and its structure. Since the 1950s, retail has had increasing access to modern techniques and technologies that have led to new options. When you compare the price levels for consumer goods in the 1950s with those of today, you will see only a small increase. But, if these prices are adjusted for inflation, you see a *de facto* reduction of over 50 per cent.

At the same time, the economy has changed from being a supplier's market to a consumer's market. Many traditional occupations and trades have experienced significant setbacks and structural changes. One result of this was an increase in the number of workers in the retail sector. In the US today, every fifth worker is involved in retail (including food services).

Although the increasing competitive pressure in retail is confronted with ever-lower profits, retail remains the central service for the future of our economic system. The use of information technology for retail is therefore vitally important, since it makes it possible to follow both major economic trends: concentration and diversification.

The current activities in retail have long since gone beyond the traditional balance of buying and selling. The services landscape of modern retail companies includes call

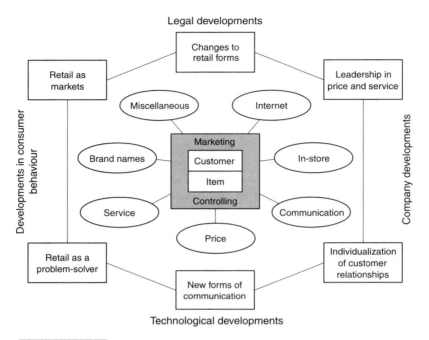

FIGURE 11.1 Activity portfolio for retail companies (© SAP AG)

centres, advertising agencies, restaurants, security services, hotels and IT services. New information and communication technologies, such as the Internet, have provided additional impetus for growth. In Germany, for example, the economic potential is far from reaching its limit.

Trends

Many retail companies today face national competition for customers and markets. With the removal of national borders through free trade agreements, the use of modern commercial technology and the exchange of data, knowledge and information all over the world in a matter of seconds with the Internet and e-mail, traditional concerns about location for these companies fade into the background. Successful retail companies purchase their products from the global marketplace and tailor the range of goods they offer to a specific region.

To better manage their assortment and location policies, companies are increasingly forced to place data about sales and consumer behaviour into large databases and exchange it with their branch locations. Partial or isolated solutions are no longer capable of fulfilling these cross-company tasks. At the same time, companies need to use more discipline to properly compare processes within a company. For this reason, each employee must be able to procure and analyse the relevant information (Fig. 11.2).

The following quotations from well-known retail specialists summarize this situation:

The lead in goods and assortment will be replaced by a lead in information.

Prof Dr Bruno Tietz, University of the Saarland (Germany)

Only the use of modern information systems will secure competitiveness in the long term.

Erwin Conradi, Board of Directors of Metro AG

The key to a market lead: move away from a functional orientation and toward consistent management of the information explosion by analysing categories according to location, sales form, and customer orientation.

Prof Dr Merkel, University of Dortmund and IMC, Mannheim (Germany)

Knowledge and information will become the supporting pillars of retail companies in the future. An 'intelligent assortment of goods' reflects the wishes of consumers and gives them additional benefits that lead to higher and more personal customer retention. The sales channel must be tailored to the demands of convenience and competence, and the segmentation of target groups must be continually improved. The use of knowledge, the provision of information, and the capture of experiential knowledge is known today as knowledge management. Enhanced technological options have made knowledge management usable and necessary for retail.

11.1.1 The Influence of New Technologies

Context

The Internet sees new companies being formed daily and at breathtaking speed. These new companies feature innovative business areas and services, not just those that provide Internet services, such as web design. All companies that develop and supply their products for a digital future fall into this category.

Consumer behaviour determines the interest retail companies show in the Internet.

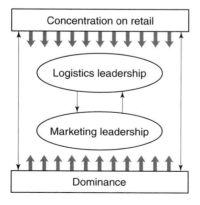

FIGURE 11.2 From logistical leadership to information leadership (© SAP AG)

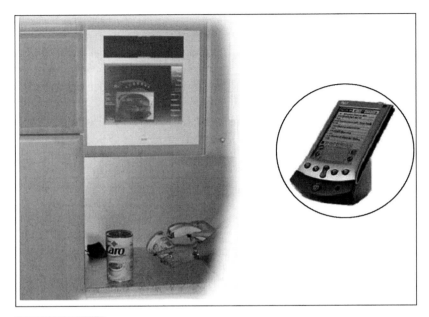

FIGURE 11.3   Consumer Direct with a handheld device (© SAP AG)

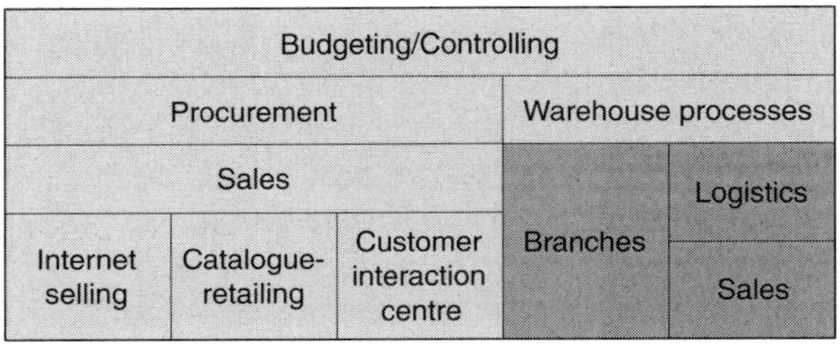

Budgeting/Controlling				
Procurement			Warehouse processes	
Sales			Branches	Logistics
Internet selling	Catalogue-retailing	Customer interaction centre		Sales

FIGURE 11.4   Unified system architecture of franchised retailers (© SAP AG)

One of the largest investments in retail involves goods distributed to several locations and hundreds of employees. The amount of revenue that can be transferred to the Internet will determine future assortment and location policies.

The future will bring with it new challenges for employees in central offices and at branch locations. Consumers are better informed and expect the higher levels of service for their business. The combination of various distribution channels plays a particularly important role. A consumer may well place an order over the Internet, return it to a branch location and still use printed catalogues to select goods. Direct consumer communication over handheld devices or self-scanning at home illustrates another example (Fig. 11.3).

11.1.2 Summary

As the industry sector with the highest number of employees, the retail industry is predestined for the use of comprehensive tools to manage the supply chain and simultaneously optimize category management. The competitive advantage will belong to companies which have set up systems to process large amounts of data and who used the Internet early on (Fig. 11.4).

11.2   THE SOLUTION FOR RETAIL COMPANIES

Integrated solution

Since it began using IT, the retail industry has always sought to reap the benefits of its software systems in accounting, human resources and logistics. Retail, with its principal components of purchasing, warehouse management and sales, offered the greatest opportunities for rationalization. These retail systems optimized typical processes, such as sales ordering or order processing.

As a leading manufacturer of commercial, client/server applications, SAP has developed a solution for the retail industry. It became available as a product, SAP Retail, in 1997. Together with well-known wholesale and retail companies from throughout the world, SAP offers a unique solution. Its retail-specific solution seamlessly links core business with accounting and human resources, enabling complete optimization of business decisions for the first time. The system maps the complete value-added chain: from the source to the consumer.

At the same time, today's mySAP Retail can be used simply and flexibly. It has a modular structure and can be implemented in steps. Its well thought-out design is its particular strength. Its data model and processes are object-oriented, upwardly compatible and reflect strong quality standards.

Multi-faceted sales channels

The system aims to map the entire supply chain from vendors to end consumers and optimize the multi-faceted procedural and control processes in the goods and information flow between vendors, retailers and consumers. In general, the structure of business processes aims at both centralized and decentralized decision-making authority. In many cases, user authorization can create an appropriate structure. However, SAP has developed material planning procedures that enable deviations from the basic approach at the level of the retail article and retail site.

A workplace for every employee

Due to the distribution of operations and tasks in a retail company, ergonomics and self-explanatory work sequences both play an important role. Process optimization requires that each employee has a system-supported, web-based workplace. Here SAP Retail provides role-based workplace templates for branch managers, distribution centre employees, buyers and retail controllers, for example. The templates also offer the company additional advantages. The web-based workplace offers more than the direct use of SAP processes. It also shortens internal and external communication and decision-making routes with its direct connection to e-mail, fax and supplementary

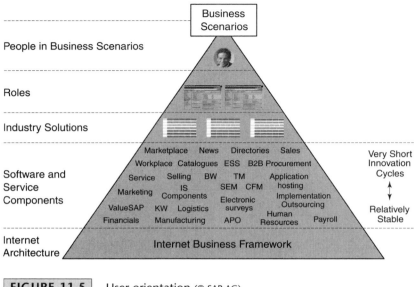

People in Business Scenarios

Roles

Industry Solutions

Software and Service Components

Internet Architecture

FIGURE 11.5 User orientation (© SAP AG)

services. In addition, employees can design their own workplaces on the computer screen (Fig. 11.5).

Preconfigured solutions

Regardless of the size of a retail company, a significant need exists for preconfigured solutions with processes for specific distribution channels. From Release 4.5 onwards, SAP Retail contains such solutions for household goods and clothing items. These solutions are simpler to install, are delivered with numerous, optimally tailored processes, and expand the industry-specific version of AcceleratedSAP (ASAP). Known as Accelerated Retail, the solutions provide process support with components for using TeamSAP.

The preconfigured solution can act as a framework for industry-specific knowledge and can provide the user with even more specialization. Some SAP hardware partners enhance Accelerated Retail with an additional configuration, called ready-to-run, that offers perfect implementation of the system for any specific hardware configuration.

11.2.1 Solution Map for Retail

The Solution Map for Retail shows the quality and range of the business processes covered by the SAP Retail Industry Solution. It includes solutions for wholesale and retail companies of every size, based upon best business practices.

Cross-industry solutions

No matter whether a company specializes in wholesale, branch operations, mail order or the hotel and restaurant sector, the Solution Map supports it by concentrating on the processes and functions that best achieve success. In this way, the company can operate with a stronger orientation to customers and markets and can react more

TABLE 11.1	Retail Solution Map			
Enterprise Management	Strategic Enterprise Management	Business Intelligence	Managerial Accounting	Financial Accounting	
Customer Relationship Management	Market Research & Analysis	Sales Support	Customer Service	Customer Loyalty	
Category Management	Collaborative Business Planning	Merchandise & Assortment Management	Product Introduction & Maintenance	Price & Promotion Management	
Procurement	Vendor Relationship Management	Forecasting & Allocation	Purchasing	Settlement	
Supply Chain Management	Distribution Planning	Inventory Management	Warehouse Management	Shipping & Transportation	Replenishment
Sales Channels	Store Business	Catalogue Sales	E-Commerce	Interactive TV	M-Commerce
Business Support	Human Resource Core Functions & Strategy	Human Resource Analytics & Enabling Solutions	Treasury/ Corporate Finance Management	Fixed Asset Management	

flexibly. The SAP Retail Solution Map can optimize the entire value-added chain and implement successful business strategies, from Category Management and Customer Relationship Management, through purchasing and supply chain management, to business processes in sales channels.

The Solution Map details how mySAP Retail approaches decisive business processes. With the integrated Data Warehouse solution, retail companies get the information they need for decisions about the strategic control and management of the organization. The mature Retail Information System (RIS) provides all business areas with the transparency they need for analyses; it contributes to efficiency in internal accounting and makes it easier to identify market trends.

The Solution Map also shows how and where mySAP Retail deals with the specific requirements of retail and clarifies the relationship between neighbouring, integrated processes in business support. Universal business processes replace traditional, department-based thinking and focus on procedures for the entire logistics chain. The Solution Map links previously isolated processes into integrated function chains.

11.2.2 Business Processes in Retail

The mySAP Retail Solution divides retail functions into seven major areas: enterprise management and business support for core business areas, CRM, Category Management, purchasing, Supply Chain and Channel Execution.

Enterprise
management

The integrated SAP Retail solution enables companies to control, plan and develop at a completely new level. The system provides the current facts and figures required to react dynamically to today's demanding and increasingly competitive markets.

SAP Strategic Enterprise Management (SAP SEM) not only gives access to current data about all the strategically important aspects of a company, but also allows this information to be used to stimulate and plan future developments. This feature enables the consolidation of results analysis and finances throughout the company – across countries and subsidiaries. mySAP Retail also supports the creation of reports for regulatory authorities, shareholders and other groups. In doing so, it takes international and local requirements into consideration.

The information needed for the correct budgeting and costing of processes, products and services is available at the press of a button. You can access profitability analyses at any level of detail.

The comprehensive accounting functions of mySAP Retail support the creation of balance sheets and other accounting reports. You can monitor vendors and customers accurately in real time, and also link them to automatic payment and debit systems. For companies operating internationally, SAP Retail offers functions such as joint venture accounting, multi-currency options and support for the euro.

The integrated Data Warehouse functions increase the efficiency and easy execution of strategic planning, controlling and monitoring processes even further. User-friendly features enable you to generate reports automatically and perform *ad hoc* data analyses that include the consideration of various user views.

Business support

mySAP Retail offers effective support for human resources, the creation of brand names and fixed assets. The functional scope includes comprehensive cash management and treasury functions.

High performance functions are available for all aspects of human resources: general management, work time and absences, travel management, wage and salary settlement, hiring and career development. You can find the right employee for the right task, and still keep an eye on performance and costs. You can also set up time-saving, self-service systems that link employees.

Comprehensive treasury functions guarantee the effective control of liquidity, investment portfolios and risks. This support includes the management of loans, interest, money market accounts and securities. Links to third-party financial systems ensure secure transactions.

In addition, mySAP Retail manages assets throughout their useful life. You can produce exact costings and budgets for important projects, and simulate and monitor depreciation and capitalization.

To support retail strategies, SAP Retail offers a complete package of proven functions, including functions for production planning, scheduling, execution, quality control and maintenance.

11.2.3 Core Business

Heterogeneous customer needs, increased pressures from competition and prices and changed market data are clear indicators of the need for retail companies to develop a new assortment policy. In light of various location factors and different customer structures, companies must always look at their strategy from new viewpoints and positions in the market.

Only integrated category analysis which covers all the responsibilities for the assortment in the retail industry can serve as the basis for true process-orientation along the value-added chain. More than ever before, the future of this process orientation will place it in a close relationship with knowledge about customers: it will demand customer relationship management (CRM).

Customer relationship management

The maintenance of customer relationships has certainly become one of the greatest challenges in the day-to-day work of retailers. mySAP Retail supports all aspects of customer relationship management with a variety of functions: market research, sales support, customer service and customer loyalty systems.

SAP provides tools with which you can use internal and external data to observe the market and determine market shares. Secondary data about competitors, such as their market share, product offerings, financial indicators and branches are also available; you can use this information for analysis or comparison. You can also judge the effectiveness of marketing campaigns and analyse sales-based data. You can then use the data to create consumer profiles for specific shopping baskets, organized by regions or other demographic factors.

A mature sales information system supports the sales force along with functions for the management of sales personnel, route planning and sales order processing. You can use performance-measurement functions with flexible key performance indicators to assess the sales force, and as the basis for determining goals.

Call centres and the Internet support customer service functions. Extra services for guarantees, returns and repairs all help to increase customer loyalty. mySAP Retail also helps to manage special service offerings such as home deliveries or wedding lists.

Today, retail companies can maintain their profit margins only when they can keep customers. mySAP Retail supports the management of loyalty programmes, customer cards and credit frameworks. You can use consumer surveys and database-supported marketing to maintain solid customer relationships.

Category management

mySAP Retail also supports the selection of appropriate articles for individual assortments and the fixing of rules for allocating inventory stocks to various branches. These features enable you to develop a competitive product strategy.

You can link external shelving optimization programmes for shelf planning and structuring to mySAP Retail and therefore ensure the most effective use of available shelving space. With a click of the mouse, you can also determine the optimum and maximum order quantities for filling shelves.

Cross-category analysis that includes consumers, distributors, vendors and the market lets you determine the most appropriate products for a category (*see* Fig. 11.6). During the process, you can focus on a specific target group. Price-analysis functions display the effects of different price strategies and contribute to competitiveness. They also indicate strategic pricing options.

At the beginning of a season you can create markdown plans for items of clothing (and specific price periods). The planning functions for price reductions let you simulate and then activate planning data. You can also compare planned and actual results for the previous period, and adjust the future price periods appropriately.

The category scorecard contains key figures that measure the efficiency of categories, including average morning indicators (GMROI), the quantity and share of overall success, the service level and profitability (Fig. 11.7).

You can also use process-cost accounting to analyse process costs, determine the order sample and compare various logistics strategies. In this manner, companies can become as efficient as possible. mySAP Retail provides a flexible, graphical workbench to maintain all planning objects. The workbench features one entry point that enables consistent top-down and bottom-up planning. It enables you to use historical data to generate planning versions integrated with financial and profitability plans.

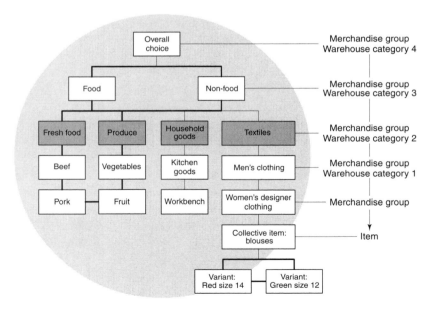

FIGURE 11.6 Category management (© SAP AG)

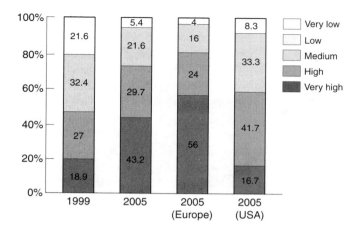

FIGURE 11.7 The future significance of category management (© SAP AG)

Procurement

Precise forecasts and the exact distribution of goods play a decisive role in a dynamically charged business world. To support the creation of precise demand forecasts, constant, trend and seasonal models, alone or together, are available. Open-to-buy (OTB) helps to plan and monitor the procurement budget. Sales, purchases and goods receipts are updated up-to-the-minute, so that you can always tell which portions of the budget have been expended and which remain available.

Allocation tables help you plan merchandise distribution and then trigger the appropriate goods movements and documents. For clothing items, a colour and size matrix simplifies the allocation of variants.

The buying functions in mySAP Retail support the daily activities of purchasing, importing and exporting. Cash flow management secures optimum liquidity for due payments and enables you to monitor cash inflows and outflows.

With mySAP Retail you can use electronic data interchange (EDI) to check incoming invoices and significantly rationalize business processes. When you post an invoice, the system immediately transfers the values to financial accounting and warehouse accounting. You can also establish agreements with vendors for the later settlement of discounts taken as volume-based rebates at the end of a period rather than with an invoice.

Supply chain management

mySAP Retail optimizes distribution processes. Investment buying tools support optimization of purchasing quantities and buying plans. The use of lot sizes, optimized order bundling, route planning and numerous additional functions can significantly help to improve delivery to branches and distribution centres.

Distribution planning helps to optimize the logistics network and evaluate different storage and distribution alternatives. You can manage and optimize internal and external sources at different levels.

Inventory management is one of the cornerstones of SAP Retail. Inventory management functions administer the total inventory of goods at a storage location along with all the corresponding valuation data. These features not only support inventories, but also provide you with the option of valuating stocks at both the delivered price and the selling price. The inventory management functions can easily handle the needs of small warehouses, so that you will not require any additional warehouse management functions.

However, more comprehensive warehouse management functions are required for complex storage locations. The warehouse management functions cover all requirements, including the ability to handle stock buffers, a transfer point or a cross-docking warehouse. You can use various strategies to manage complex warehouse structures, storage bins, different storage types, such as high rack storage areas or bulk storage, storage placement and storage removal.

The shipping and transportation components cover all the processes required for goods issue: picking, packing, loading and transportation. Efficient transportation planning and processing ensures that shipments go out without delays, arrive on time and that the associated costs remain as low as possible. The features reduce the percentage of a product's price that is due to delivery costs and therefore further increase competitiveness.

You can base your replenishment strategies upon sales or inventory data. In both cases, extremely flexible forecast functions are available. The vendor-managed inventory functions for vendor-carried stocks help vendors to plan the stocks of their products at retail locations.

Distribution channels

The high numbers of personnel employed at branches results in extremely cost-intensive processes. But the closeness to the customer at branch locations also offers unique opportunities for long-term and lucrative customer relationships. The central functions of mySAP Retail have been enhanced and configured into SAP Retail Store – a separate system for retail sales at branches. The browser-based interface operates intuitively and is user-friendly; it requires only minimal training to operate. SAP Retail Store features links to the central SAP Retail system and thus enables branches to profit from its efficient optimization and personnel planning functions. In addition, seamless integration into every area provides all the functions required for personnel settlement.

Certified interfaces can link external POS (point of sale) systems to mySAP Retail so that all retail business processes undergo processing in a completely integrated, stand-alone system. mySAP Retail also features comprehensive audit functions for receipts that check, correct and process the detailed sales data from cash registers.

By their very nature, the business processes in wholesale and in agency business (central regulation) are complicated, particularly regarding those stored in the logistics chain. mySAP Retail provides wholesalers with all the key functions they need for customer and order management: key account management, contact management, order monitoring and invoicing, management of rebates and the integration of sales and purchasing. In addition, mySAP Retail offers complete support for agency business, for central regulation processes and for factoring processes.

FIGURE 11.8   Some popular Internet shopping sites (© SAP AG)

The use of new, electronic media has breathed new life into mail order and catalogue sales. Online shopping and telesales have opened new doors for many companies, but the traditional printed catalogue still remains one of the key elements of a mail order business. A detailed database that can address targeted customers as individuals and as groups is essential for success, whether the sale occurs wholly over the Internet or from a catalogue.

SAP Online Store enables companies to sell products over the world wide web. In addition to presenting products in web catalogues, the application offers all the functions and processes required for sales and distribution. These functions include virtual shopping baskets, customer registration, secure payment procedures and order monitoring. Fig. 11.8 shows some of the most popular Internet shopping sites.

mySAP Retail also provides a comprehensive suite of services tailored to the needs of the hotel and restaurant industry. The functional scope of such services ranges from menu planning, previewing and management to functions for preparing meals, managing restaurant personnel and POS (point of sale) management.

11.2.4 Further Development

SAP will consistently continue to develop and improve the comprehensive functions of its mySAP Retail Industry Solution. It will pay particular attention to improved performance, so that the solution can cover the significantly increased information requirement for customer segmentation.

The EnjoySAP Initiative marked a further milestone and was delivered with Release 4.6. It offers improved usability, focused on the needs of users. The SAP Workplace, a result of the mySAP.com Internet initiative, provides all the functions required by retail companies in function-specific roles.

New procedures are being implemented as part of implementation projects, such as rack jobbing or customer card applications. A shared project with Roland Berger in London to create templates for category management illustrates a special focus on the improvement of the strategic abilities of the system.

11.3   SAMPLE APPLICATION

Enterprise profile

The Vendex Food Group is part of Vendex International (V.I.) N.V. which has its head-quarters in Helmond, the Netherlands. The Vendex Food Group operates grocery stores and runs the following distribution chains in the Netherlands:

- Basis market
- Convenience: Dagmarkt and Zentrum Supermarket
- ESM: full line supermarket
- Konmar: self-service warehouse
- Pet's Place: speciality store for pets

The distribution chain in Belgium includes the following:

- Battard: supermarket
- Echo: supermarket
- Eda: discount store

The firm owns a share in Radar Food and works in the Eurogroup together with BML (Austria), Co-op (Switzerland) and Rewe (Germany). In 1996, with its 17,000 employees, the company enjoyed net revenues of about $2 billion.

In 1996, the Vendex Food Group had 818 branches, with a total sales area of 500,000 m^3, with eleven distribution centres, five meat packing centres and three centres for fruits and vegetables.

The situation prior to implementation

Some 1,500 functions had been defined. The distribution channels wanted to develop a new, uniform system. The alternatives under discussion included the following:

- Upgrading the legacy systems
- Specialized programs
- An integrated system

The decision for SAP Retail

The Vendex Food Group eventually decided that 'SAP Retail as an information system is one of the pillars that guarantees the future success of the enterprise'. The SAP Industry Solution will enable the Dutch company to meet the following goals:

▓ By working together with its vendors, satisfy customer wishes even better now and in the future

▓ To advance in retail sales by using new management methods, supported by the most up-to-date information technology

▓ To offer employees the opportunity to advance further, develop further and to improve the company's results

▓ To give shareholders a good return

Significance in enterprise policy

The implementation of SAP Retail has the following goals:

▓ Establishment of a warehouse management system integrated with financial accounting and a management information system

▓ A user-friendly system

▓ The greatest possible independence for distribution channels

▓ The ability to better address consumers' needs, and thus improve profits

▓ Flexible support of expansion efforts

▓ Make it possible to use management by exception

▓ Open structure for hardware and software

Some 70 software companies were preselected according to specific criteria. The Vendex Food Group decided on SAP for the following reasons:

▓ It included coverage of the functions they needed

▓ Its high level of integration with other retail functions

▓ User-friendliness

▓ Flexibility

▓ Openness to external applications (Spaceman, MS Office and so on)

References

Joachim Hertel (1997) *Warenwirtschaftssysteme: Grundlagen und Konzepte*, Physica.

Bruno Tietz (1993) *Der Handelsbetrieb*, Verlag Franz Vahlen.

Joachim Zentes (1999) *Marketing für Handelsunternehmen: SAP-Studie im Rahmen der Entwicklungsplanung*, Walldorf.

mySAP Service Providers Industry Solution

Christa Koppe and Dr Martin Przewloka, SAP AG

12.1 A GROWING INDUSTRY

Markets

Contrary to the trend in other industries, service providers have enjoyed constant, and in some areas meteoric, growth. Ninety per cent of the firms founded in Germany between 1976 and 1992 were service providers. In only ten years, between 1984 and 1994, this sector of the economy created 3.2 million new jobs. The term 'service provider' covers a multi-faceted landscape of companies. Service providers include advertising agencies, accounting firms, management consultants, engineering companies, call centres, security agencies, IT services and temp agencies; an almost endless list. New information and communications technologies such as the Internet have given the industry additional impetus for growth. In Germany, for example, the economic potential of this innovative tertiary sector is far from being exhausted.

Trends

Today, many companies face international competition for customers and markets. With the removal of national borders, particularly in Europe, the use of modern commercial technologies and the worldwide exchange of data, knowledge and information in seconds have made traditional concerns about locations almost meaningless for these firms. Successful service providers think and work globally; they tailor their services to specific regions. The electronic marketplaces of the Internet often offer new services from the very first day of availability, and thus immediately experience worldwide competition.

TABLE 12.1	Future markets for service providers (Bullinger 1998, p. 8)
Push and Pull Factors	Areas of Growth
Optimization of Service Offerings	Business Services (Facility Management, R&D, Consulting and Security)
Knowledge of Production Factors	Brokerage/Mediation (Work, Information and Goods)
Technological Advances	Media and Telecommunications (Multimedia Business Services and External Consulting)
Just-In-Time, Cocooning	Mobility and Logistics (Intermodal Mobility Services and Home Delivery)
Economic Environmentalism	Ecology (Recycling, Prevention and Control and Trades)
Individual Life Provisions	Financial Services (Non-Banking) (One-stop financial services and Income Planning)
Demography, Wellness	Social and Health Services (Emergency Care, Fitness and Coverage of Catastrophes)
Convenience, Fun	Leisure and Recreation (Leisure and Recreation Centres, Do-It-Yourself, NGOs and Building)

In the future, production and service offerings will grow together even more strongly. The provision of services also has increasing importance for production companies, as an integral or complementary part of their business. Services provided before during, and after production processes offer individual solutions to problems. These services increasingly count among the core competencies of industry. Car manufacturers provide a good example. No longer do their products, vehicles, stand in the foreground. That place has been taken by the service of mobility that the products provide (Bullinger 1997, p. 35).

For example, 'the future world of work will be characterized by an intelligent combination of industry and service providers', says Jürgen E. Schrempp, chairman of DaimlerChrysler AG. The chair of Aachener und Münchener Versicherung AG, Elmo Freiherr von Schorlemer, sees 'the goals have been set: away from a functional orientation, and towards a service orientation for products, sales and maintenance'.

Knowledge and information will form the essential components of service providers in the future. 'Intelligent service' responds to differentiated wishes and creates new, enhanced benefits for customers. The product itself might be intelligent, or marketed as a supplemental service. The ability to deal with knowledge, to make information available and to use the value of experience together defines knowledge management. It is another key ability of successful service providers.

12.1.1 The Influence of New Technologies

It is sometimes said that one calendar year equals seven Internet years. This comparison highlights the tremendous speed of innovation that companies must match in the Internet Age. But increasing the 'stroke rate' is not enough: the digital world demands new structures and processes. Effective service-provider management creates the preconditions for those needs. In an age of global computer networking, virtual structures continually take on new roles. This approach includes the optimum use of internal and external resources.

The use of innovative technologies enables companies to integrate employees, inside or outside the firm, into their processes, and without considering location or time. Teams from various companies can communicate and work together across all borders. These kinds of virtual structures can quickly join together multi-faceted core competencies, to create both efficient synergies and top-level service for customers (Fig. 12.1).

Employees now face new challenges. The readiness to transfer information and knowledge is a necessity for the success of any virtual group or team. The qualifications expected in this situation by service providers include the following: the ability to assume responsibility, work independently, quality assurance, the confidence to deal with information, familiarity with media, team orientation and creative thinking (Bullinger 1997, p. 55).

High-tech service providers face both opportunities and risks. In many sectors, technological change leads to reduced workforces, but in other sectors, the same change creates the potential for new service providers and jobs.

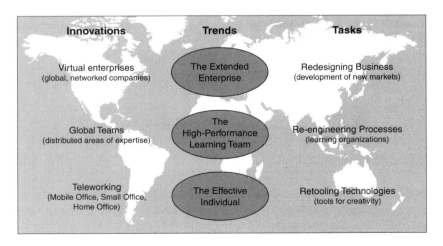

Innovations	Trends	Tasks
Virtual enterprises (global, networked companies)	The Extended Enterprise	Redesigning Business (development of new markets)
Global Teams (distributed areas of expertise)	The High-Performance Learning Team	Re-engineering Processes (learning organizations)
Teleworking (Mobile Office, Small Office, Home Office)	The Effective Individual	Retooling Technologies (tools for creativity)

FIGURE 12.1 | Service-provider management for optimum inclusion of resources (Bullinger 1997, p. 51) (© SAP AG)

12.1.2 Summary

In Germany, there is great scope for further economic development in the service provider industry. Accordingly, the future demands that service providers develop new products with an orientation to new customers and benefits. How companies adjust their organizational structure and the creation of service processes to changing conditions will be decisive factors in their success.

12.2　THE SOLUTION FOR SERVICE PROVIDERS

Integrated
solutions

Many companies oriented toward providing services already work successfully with SAP R/3. Most significantly, back-office applications, such as financial accounting or human resources, play an important role during the implementation of SAP standard software. SAP has long known that service providers, in particular, require comprehensive functions that must map the entire business in a completely integrated environment. These goals led to the development of a process-oriented solution for service providers, the SAP Service Provider Industry Solution. In close collaboration with ten pilot customers from companies representing consulting, accounting, software development, temp agencies, outsourcing, advertising and technical services, SAP first undertook significant enhancements in the creation of master data. In addition, it also introduced new applications to confirm time worked, to handle invoicing and for reporting. Implementation of SAP R/3 Release 3.1 showed the extremely high performance of the enhancements. An improved and expanded version of SAP Service Provider was deliv-

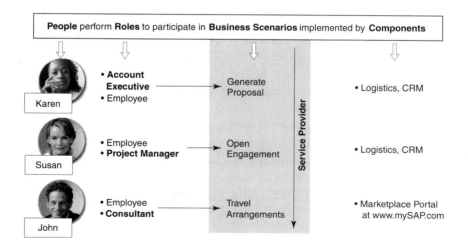

FIGURE 12.2　Roles and business scenarios (© SAP AG)

ered worldwide with Release 4.5. As a result, SAP gained a large number of customers from the service provider industry.

A workplace for each employee

Besides the familiar process-oriented use of SAP R/3 a need exists today to provide each employee with a system-supported, web-based workplace: the mySAP Workplace. It offers employees the functions they need to perform their company-specific roles: as technicians, accountants, sales agents or project managers. The web-based Workplace offers more than the direct use of SAP processes. It also shortens internal and external communication and decision-making routes with its direct connection to e-mail, fax and additional services. In addition, employees can design their own workplaces on the computer screen (*see* Fig. 12.2).

Preconfigured solutions

SAP has recently gone yet another step further. A significant need exists, particularly for small and medium-sized companies, for preconfigured solutions with processes specific to service providers. From Release 4.5 onwards, SAP Service Provider now provides, for the first time, such a solution with a comprehensive number of preconfigured processes. SAP has enhanced the solution with an industry-specific version of AcceleratedSAP (ASAP) as a process-oriented component for the use of TeamSAP, known as Best Practices for Service Providers. This preconfigured solution offers a framework upon which to place industry-specific knowledge and enables users to specialize. Several customers have already successfully implemented Best Practices for Service Providers.

12.2.1 Solution Map for Service Providers

A look at the Solution Map of SAP Service Provider (*see* Table 12.2) clarifies the processes and functions.

Cross-industry solution

The design of the Service Provider Solution Map follows consistently process-oriented use, regardless of the area in which a given service provider operates. It displays the enhanced offering against the background of solutions with industry-dependent and independent specifics for enterprise management, customer relationship management and business support. The life cycles of a typical service provider company act as an example. The Solution Map shows how to use the main processes (sales and marketing, project and resource management, field service, out-sourcing and invoicing) completely, partially, or in combination, depending upon the business transaction. For example, a typical, lean service provider scenario can include the functions of contract management, activity input (confirmation of times and expenses), and various invoicing methods (based on fixed costs or actual expenses).

12.2.2 A Typical Business Transaction

Acquisition and quotation phase

SAP Service Provider supports service provider companies in every business phase (Fig. 12.3). Even during acquisition, a company has a comprehensive palette of process categories available: sales and marketing, project management, resource management and customer relationship management. At an early stage, a company can evaluate the

TABLE 12.2 Service Providers Solution Map

Enterprise Management	Strategic Enterprise Management	Business Intelligence	Managerial Accounting	Financial Accounting	Sales Channels	Service Agreements	Service Fulfillment
Customer Relationship Management	Customer Service	Marketing Program Management	Sales Management	Sales Cycle Management	Customer Care		
Sales	Acquisition	Order Management	Contract Management	Planning & Simulation			
Project Management	Project Planning	Project Execution & Monitoring	Activity Recording	Travel Management	Strategic Reporting	Customer Care	
Resource Management	Recruitment	Training & Certification	Labour Resource Planning	Customer Care			
Knowledge Management	Historical Data Management	Knowledge Development	Knowledge Transfer				
Field Service	Call Management	Scheduling & Dispatching	Maintenance	Customer Care			
Business Process Outsourcing	IT	Financials	Logistics	Human Resources	Customer Care		
Billing	Billing Plan	Fixed Price Billing	Resource Related Billing Billing				
Business Support	Human Resource Core Functions & Strategy	Human Resource Analytics & Enabling Solutions	Procurement	Treasury Management	Fixed Asset Management		

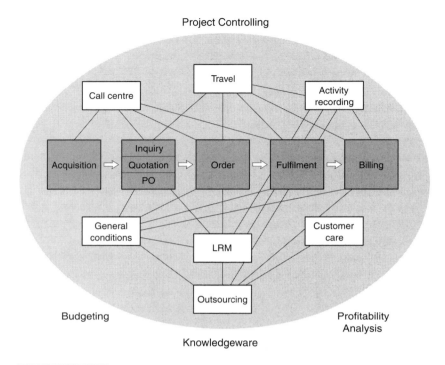

Project Controlling

Budgeting

Profitability Analysis

Knowledgeware

FIGURE 12.3 Processing a business transaction by a service provider (© SAP AG)

business area, plan marketing activities and respond to customer needs. The service provider can choose to make use of historical, current or competitor data. Supported by the system, the second step is for a company to offer a quotation to the customer. It can also supplement the process with detailed planning of time, costs, revenue and resources (labour resource management or LRM).

Service provider orders

If the quotation is accepted, the type and complexity of the business plays no role as it undergoes processing in the SAP Service Provider. The software always offers a suitable solution, whether it is for lean processing with the functionally powerful SAP Sales & Distribution application component or for complex applications with SAP Project System (PS). The components and functions of service management are completely integrated, particularly when processing a service from a highly technical service provider, such as those of engineering services or facility management. Whether the deal came from the initiative of the service provider or the customer is insignificant.

Planning, simulation and budgeting of the business or individual steps enhance the solution portfolio. The definition of workflow scenarios can automate processing. For example, the system can send e-mails containing information about responsibilities and employees directly related to the procedure.

Confirmation

Confirmation functions (timesheets and travel costs) support a service provider during order processing. The solution also provides procedures such as individual or centralized entry, confirmations that require approval as well as those that do not, and confirmations via modems, intranet or Internet. SAP Service Provider makes all these types of confirmation available in a role-based workplace.

Billing

Service providers frequently make significant demands on billing systems. The spectrum is broad: current billing, billing according to effort, billing according to a fixed price (with or without consideration of milestones, periodically, or irregularly), advance billing, or down-payment requests. SAP Service Provider provides a comprehensive scope of functions that enables flexible decision-making: billing at an aggregate level, by day or employee, and with or without consideration of approval procedures. At each level, you can decide the scope of billing, and whether it is to take place immediately or later.

Collective transfer postings

Companies often need to perform transfer postings of confirmations such as time and expenses. In some cases, hours originally posted to a project not intended for billing may need to be transferred to a billable project. SAP Service Provider enables global transfer postings in this case.

Reporting

Throughout the entire life cycle of a project, SAP Service Provider contains comprehensive order-specific and organizational reporting functions. Multi-faceted profitability analyses with various valuation procedures (determination of work in process with a revenue orientation, cost orientation, percentage of completion and so on) at any time and at any level round out the functions. Through process mapping, SAP Service Provider consistently receives information about employee salaries from options that define employee-specific sales revenues, profitability evaluations and activity reports. Here, too, SAP Service Provider delivers preconfigured, role-based solutions.

12.2.3 Future Development

SAP will continue to improve the comprehensive functions of its SAP Service Provider Industry solution together with pilot customers. The EnjoySAP initiative, implemented in Release 4.6, has set another milestone for user-friendly operability. Development in 2000 focused on a completely integrated Labor Resource Management System (LRM) and creating off-line scenarios for time and expense notifications. It also worked on a transfer-price concept for procedure-oriented parallel depiction and holding of valuation rates from an enterprise, legal and transfer-price view, and on the further development of a time sheet. SAP will also offer industry-specific training in the future, to inform the various service provider sectors about the Service Provider solution by using typical procedures as examples.

12.3   TWO SAMPLE APPLICATIONS

Two examples clarify how the scenario described above can be implemented in practice.

Consulting and auditing

A large, international consulting and auditing firm needed a completely integrated environment to map its business. The required areas included back-office functions such as financial accounting and human resources. The firm also required mapping of the front-office business for enterprise consulting, taxes and auditing. The enterprise operated as several legally distinct entities that frequently exchanged services with each other, sometimes across company codes.

The enterprise placed great value on lean processing in the context of master data creation and therefore decided to use the Sales & Distribution (SD) application component for central creation of clients, orders and projects. The firm also required decentralized creation, billing and profitability-oriented order management. The items on the service provider order that had been tailored to company-specific requirements had to record the type and value of the order at a high level: the hectic nature of the business does not often permit entry of detailed orders at the time of creation. When an order came in, the company could already determine if the business involved actual or fixed-price billing. During the life cycle of the order, however, the variants had to be able to change.

All office-based personnel and sales personnel had to be included in confirmations. The company decided against the implementation of an approval procedure and against centralized entry. The first step set up online and intranet confirmations: the company is considering an off-line scenario for the future.

The guiding principle was the timely billing of services: the company wanted to drastically reduce receivables and improve its liquidity. In a two-level design the first step was to create the invoice as an approval template and then, after approval, to process, post and send it. The design involved recording order and confirmation-specific details on the invoice. As desired, the decision to bill can be made by exact day and employee. Employee-related sales prices can be maintained by orders and billed accordingly.

Reporting consistently continues this employee-related approach. Employee and employee-specific group reports, evaluations and key performance indicators (KPI) can be represented in Profitability Analysis (CO-PA) now and in the Business Information Warehouse (BW) in the future.

The company is currently working on further uses of the Business Information Warehouse. All project managers are to have access to these functions at their workplaces. This design should provide each project manager with the required evaluations and key performance indicators according to orders for every phase of the project. SAP Service Provider also provides well thought-out and highly developed solutions for reporting on key performance indicators.

Technical services   Implementation at a medium-sized company took a different approach. This firm is a legally independent service unit of a large German car company. Its core business involves construction services (bodies, transmissions and chassis) for the motor industry.

The service provider implemented the Project System (PS) application component: design phase, construction phase and assembly phase distinguished projects from each other. The use of networks that include milestones, budgeting and resource planning is planned for the future. The important nodes for billing with the work breakdown structure are linked to customer order items in the Sales & Distribution (SD) application component.

Decentralized entry of services (employee hours) and timely, expense-based billing play an essential role for this car service provider. For each project, the company must also invoice customers for additional services, expenses and products such as travel costs, software rental and leasing fees. Depending upon the agreement with the customer, these costs are calculated exactly, shared or surcharged. In this context, SAP Service Provider offers billing functions that enable the relevant employees to integrate all their decisions through one interface. The decisions involved include billing current, returned or refused quantities and values, changes and the application of conditions. The company is decentralizing its currently centralized controlling operations in steps. The company also intends to implement Profitability Analysis (CO-PA) and Profit Centre Accounting.

References

Hans-Jörg Bullinger (Ed.) (1997) *Dienstleistung für das 21. Jahrhundert: Gestaltung des Wandels und Aufbruch in die Zukunft*, Stuttgart.

Hans-Jörg Bullinger (Ed.) (1998) *Dienstleistung 2000plus – Zukunftsreport Dienstleistungen in Deutschland*, Stuttgart.

Index